CREDIT RISK AND EXPOSURE IN SECURITIZATION AND TRANSACTIONS

Also by T. H. Donaldson and published by Macmillan

HOW TO HANDLE PROBLEM LOANS
LENDING IN INTERNATIONAL COMMERCIAL BANKING
THE MEDIUM-TERM LOAN MARKET (*with J. A. Donaldson*)
THINKING ABOUT CREDIT
UNDERSTANDING CORPORATE CREDIT

Credit Risk and Exposure in Securitization and Transactions

T. H. Donaldson, FCIB

M
MACMILLAN

First published 1989

Published by
THE MACMILLAN PRESS LTD
Houndmills, Basingstoke, Hampshire RG21 2XS
and London
Companies and representatives
throughout the world

Typeset by Footnote Graphics,
Warminster, Wilts

Printed in Hong Kong

British Library Cataloguing in Publication Data
Donaldson, T. H., *1936–*
Credit risk and exposure in securitization
and transactions.
1. Great Britain. Banks. Lending. Control
I. Title
332.1′753′0941
ISBN 0–333–47050–8

Contents

PART IV RISK/REWARD

List of Glossary Items

Figures refer to the chapters in which words or phrases are explained.

Acknowledgements

The usual but nonetheless heartfelt thanks to my family for their forbearance while I was writing this book.

My thanks to my colleagues, Gordon McKechnie and Rene Poisson, for reading and commenting on parts of the book. And to Morgan Guaranty for enabling me to acquire the experience on which the book is based.

Despite the above, the views and mistakes, if any, in the book are mine and mine alone.

T. H. DONALDSON

1 Introduction

GLOSSARY

Borrower The beneficiary of a credit risk taken by another without any reciprocal risk. This includes the borrower of a conventional bank loan, or the issuer of a bond or similar instrument.

Commercial bank A bank which originated by taking deposits and lending money to others at its own risk. It also provided services inherent to this main function, such as money transmission.

Counterparty Party to a transaction in which each side accepts a credit risk on the other; the credit risk is often not a key aspect of the transaction. Foreign exchange and swaps are two examples of counterparty transactions.

Credit risk The risk of loss because a borrower/counterparty fails to meet its obligations. Failure may reflect financial problems and ultimately bankruptcy; or an unethical or near fraudulent refusal to meet obligations which are morally due, but not legally enforceable.

(Dis)intermediation Commercial banks intermediate by standing between depositors and borrowers. Disintermediation is the reverse process whereby loans which were previously made by banks are financed directly by the investor/depositor, often by buying securities.

Investment bank A bank, often in origin a stockbroker, the core of whose business is to make markets in securities, both debt and equity, and to assist companies in raising funds through the securities markets, often by underwriting them. Investment and commercial banks are prevented by US law from encroaching on each other's territory, but this division has been challenged in the 1980s. In most other countries it has either never been as clear-cut, or was a matter of custom rather than law. In these countries the distinction has broken down rather faster.

Merchant bank In origin, a merchant which allowed other merchants to use its credit standing by accepting a bill of exchange (hence the importance of the Accepting Houses among merchant banks). It developed to cover much the same ground as the (mainly US) investment banks; however, the different origin and legal background gave a different orientation and some commercial banking aspects. Since October 1986 merchant banks have been able to buy stockbrokers or be members of the Stock Exchange, so that the differences are reducing. The phrase also describes the specialised subsidiaries of US commercial banks, established to perform investment banking overseas. Finally US investment banks call it 'merchant banking' when they make large bridging loans to help clients fund acquisitions.

Securitization The process of replacing bank loans with various forms of security and of changing the form of bank loans so that they become more easily transferable and take on other aspects of a security. Floating rate notes, NIFs and eurocommercial paper are examples.

Upfront payment A payment at or near the beginning of a transaction which extends over a longer time. Examples include underwriting or participation fees, payable at the signing of a loan, and contrasting with commitment and utilisation fees which are paid over its life in relation to usage or availability, or a single payment in the early days of a swap which is offset by a stream of payments the other way.

DEVELOPMENTS IN SUBSTITUTES AND SUPPLEMENTS FOR LENDING

Traditionally, companies needing finance had three sources. For short- and more recently medium-term requirements they could look to the banking system; for longer-term debt requirements they could look either to a public bond market or to private placements; and for equity to the stock exchange or to family or institutional shareholders. The importance and strength of each market varied from country to country, as did the extent to which governments provided, regulated or inhibited various types of finance. The three types of finance were supplied by different bodies with little overlap or competition between them. In some countries, most notably the United States, there were legal provisions to ensure that this was true.

The separation between the markets began to break down in the 1960s and 1970s. High interest rates inhibited customers from borrowing long-term fixed rate money through the bond market; American banks moving abroad found American and other companies who wanted medium- or long-term money for use outside their country of origin. Commercial banks, from the early 1960s onwards, could increasingly provide this through the euromarkets. Following the introduction of 'Competition and Credit Control' in 1972, banks also began to provide medium-term sterling funds (two to ten years, but mostly in the five to seven year range) to UK borrowers; similar practices developed in other countries over the following decade. As high interest rates and exchange controls made domestic bond issues unattractive and international ones unavailable, medium-term bank debt became the main alternative to short-term debt and equity.

In the late 1960s/early 1970s the eurobond market began to offer an alternative source of funds. At first it offered only fixed rate dollars, in modest amounts and for medium-term maturities. As it grew it offered larger amounts for longer maturities (twelve to fifteen years) and in different currencies. Until the late 1970s, however, the eurobond market was seen more as a supplementary source of types of finance which commercial banks could not offer, than as a competitor.

In the late 1970s the floating rate note (FRN) began to provide direct competition to medium-term bank loans. It was followed in the early 1980s by the revolving underwriting facility (RUF) and the note issuance facility (NIF). The chief difference between these was in the issuing mechanism: the RUF was designed to give most of the profits to the investment bank which arranged the facility and dealt in the notes; the NIF to give more to the commercial banks, which in both cases provided the underlying commitment which allowed companies to sell short-term notes as part of a medium-term financing. NIFs and RUFs led on to MOFs (multi option facilities), ECP (eurocommercial paper) and EMTNs (euro medium-term notes). All these facilities were cheaper than conventional bank facilities for three main reasons. They were liquid, which made them more attractive to banks and opened a wider investor market; they provided investment banks with a fee without taking a commercial banking risk, and thus gave an incentive to outnegotiate commercial banks desperate for assets; and they changed the form of risk, sometimes by taking it off balance sheet; this allowed eager participants to believe that the risk was lower than a loan and thus justified lower pricing.

Commercial banks thus found that they were lending less at lower rates and to weaker credits than before. They fought back by trying to become investment banks, and seeking products where commercial banks had a continuing advantage. This raised competition in many types of investment banking to a level at least as cut-throat as the investment banks had brought into commercial banking. It also led to several new generic types of product, as well as numerous minor variants of existing products.

The generic types included currency and interest rate swaps, which allowed companies to change the nature of their borrowing and to tap markets in which they would otherwise have no interest. Warrants, options, futures and variants such as caps and collars also allowed borrowers either to transform or hedge risks, and thus to borrow in ways that would previously have seemed unsound.

This book is concerned mainly with the resulting changes in the nature of credit risk. Banks and borrowers both find themselves taking risks the nature of which is not obvious. Sometimes they may fail to recognize a risk at all; at others they may think they are taking a trading risk when in fact it is a credit risk or vice versa. Thus credit risk is more closely interwoven with other types of risk than before, and more easily confused with them; lending bankers need to understand more about these other types than in the past, and other types of banker need to understand more about credit.

Securitization and disintermediation have thus changed the nature of banking risk, and also changed the people who are taking the risks. In some cases the risk is less, in others greater, in yet others it depends on the precise circumstances. It is clear, however, that the risks are less well understood, both by the people taking them and by those selling them or advising about them. Even risks which are inherently less than normal banking risks can cause problems if they are not properly understood.

THE DIFFERENCE BETWEEN BORROWER/ COUNTERPARTY RISK AND TRANSACTION RISK

A traditional bank lender normally makes the strength of the borrower the main basis for a decision as to whether to lend. Naturally he takes account of the nature of the loan, the reason for which the borrower needs it, the sources of repayment and so on; but these are mainly ways of assessing the borrower's strength. As long as the borrower remains sound it will meet its obligations.

Even with traditional bank lending there are some cases where the nature of the transaction is more important. Self liquidating commodity financing is one example; project lending another; and there are many others. In a few cases, the bank has no recourse to the borrower's general assets if the transaction being financed fails; these are pure transaction risks. They are also the exception. In bank loans, the transaction may be the first line of defence; if it fails the bank looks to the general assets and earnings of the borrower for repayment. Of course, if a bank will only lend on a fully secured self liquidating basis, this may throw doubt on the value of recourse to the borrower, but banks rarely finance even sound transactions for borrowers they do not expect to survive. Admittedly they sometimes pay less attention to the borrower's chances of survival than, arguably, they should.

Most of the concern, and lack of understanding, about the new or securitized transaction focuses – or fails to focus – on the risks of the transaction. In so far as the risk is other than credit, this may be fully justified. There is a real danger, however, that investment bankers or dealers focus so much on covering the trading or other risks that they overlook the credit risk.

Equally it is easy for a lending banker to assume that the transaction risk of a swap or an underwritten NIF or RUF is the same or less than for a comparable loan. Quite often this is close to the truth, and the banker avoids serious punishment. However, many of the instruments under review are so new that few if any have yet run their course, so that we do not know with any accuracy what sort of failure level to expect. But the risks of transactions vary from those of a normal loan in several ways. The most important variations are not related to credit at all, but to changes in interest rates, currencies or other prices. In some cases they improve the credit standing of the borrower/counterparty, in others they can weaken it; many transactions do not affect the risk of loss, but only the size.

The risks of an interest rate swap, for instance, vary with the level of interest rates in the currency concerned, those of a currency swap with both the interest rates and the volatility of exchange rates between the currencies. A banker who ignores these variations runs two risks, and may unnecessarily or unknowingly accept both of them in different cases. On the one hand he may accept a risk that is greater than that of a loan, without recognizing the extent or nature of the extra risk; on the other he may turn down a better risk, or one which helps to protect existing exposure, because he does not recognize the benefits.

A particular difference between a normal lending risk and many, though not all, transaction risks is that the latter are often reciprocal. When a bank enters into an interest rate or currency swap with a counterparty, each runs a similar risk if the other fails. This is not true with loans; the borrower, once he has his money, runs no direct risk if the bank fails. Some transactions such as foreign exchange have always been reciprocal, but, with the variety of new instruments, the reciprocal element has become more important to non-bank counterparties; many of the instruments involve longer maturities than the normal forward exchange contract, again making the reciprocal element more important; and the credit standing of all but a few of the very strongest banks has declined both absolutely and in relation to the best corporate credits. This has weakened the already poor ability of banks to build protection into their agreements. It is one thing to ask for tight covenants, cross default or even collateral in a loan; quite another in a swap when the counterparty can reasonably say: 'Certainly, if you give me the same; my credit rating is, after all, as high as, or higher than, yours.'

THE NEED TO IDENTIFY AND UNDERSTAND THE DIFFERENT RISKS

Historically the risks in commercial banking were kept fairly distinct from each other. The banker who decided that it was safe to give Company X an overdraft or term loan assessed the risk that Company X could pay. Treasury made sure that the bank could fund the asset, and where appropriate decided whether to match fund it or take an interest rate risk in the hope of an additional profit. The same was true, *mutatis mutandis*, of foreign exchange transactions. It was even truer of the difference between lending risk and underwriting risk; most commercial banks did no underwriting, and investment banks no lending. Similar comments applied to most of the other types of risk which banks take and which are discussed in later chapters.

Today however these comments are either not true at all or are heavily qualified. Commercial banks, directly or through subsidiaries, are in the underwriting business, in some cases in new forms, in others competing with the investment banks in security underwriting. Investment banks in turn are beginning to take credit risk, sometimes in diluted forms but increasingly in direct, if narrowly focused, competition with commercial banks. Within each type of bank too the distinctions between different types of risk taken are in danger of becoming blurred. The banker no longer just lends, but buys and sells loans; the treasurer no longer just funds assets provided to him by the banker, but seeks profitable assets himself – assets which carry a credit risk. In due course banks will reshape their organizations to ensure that the proper types and levels of experience are brought to bear on each risk; the process has already started. Meanwhile, however, the risks are being taken and banks need to ensure that those responsible under the present organization understand all types of risk and recognize them when they crop up in new or unexpected forms. This is necessary to avoid unsound risks in the short run, and to ensure that the evolving organization is sound and staffed by properly qualified people.

In addition, some new products involve a mixture of risks which no one discipline in traditional banking fully covers. To take a simple example, an interest swap involves two risks. The more important, to the swap trader, is the trading risk, at least when the bank is taking positions, not simply acting as a go-between in matching positions. However there is also a credit risk; if the counterparty fails the bank will find itself with the opposite trading risk to the one it thought it was taking. Swap traders will ensure that the trading risk is reasonable on the assumption that all parties to the swap meet their obligations. The validity of the assumption is a matter of credit judgement. Most swap dealers' interest in credit is small.

Most banks require swaps to be approved by a banking or credit officer familiar with the counterparty. However banks are increasingly doing one-off deals, profitable in themselves, with counterparties with which they have no other relationship. Even where this is not the case, anecdotal evidence suggests that the requirement for credit approval is too often overlooked or treated as a formality. Moreover, while the risk on a straightforward swap is well documented, and understood by a growing number of bankers, there are many variations. These may not change the trading risk, or may do so only to a minor extent and in ways which swap traders understand. Sometimes they change the credit risk.

For instance, some swaps have mismatched payments; the mismatch may be short and the amount small, reflecting the different ways of setting interest in different markets. Or it may be a larger differential, perhaps an upfront payment on one side offset by lower interest payments over five or ten years on the other, with payments present valued. The swap risk is not significantly changed, but, unless the dealer recognizes the credit impact of the difference, he may well present it to the credit officer as a normal swap. Unless the credit officer knows enough to ask the right questions, he in turn may approve it without realizing the true extent of the risk the bank is taking.

It may be argued that this often does not matter. A company whose credit is good for a five-year swap is probably also good for a smaller five-year amortizing loan. This will be true in many cases. But there are three reasons why this is an unsound and, in the long run, dangerous argument. First, the counterparty sometimes wants the upfront payment because it cannot borrow money any other way; the payment is therefore a concealed loan which other banks have judged as unsound. Secondly banks make many credit decisions, and however good their systems and judgement, some are bound to go wrong. Where the counterparty with the upfront payment is one of these the bank would probably lose money anyway, but now may lose more than it allowed for when accepting the risk. And thirdly, banks get paid for taking risks in relation to the total amount that they can lose and to the likelihood of loss. Where they misjudge either of these factors they are paid too little to compensate for the inevitable losses they will have somewhere in their portfolio. The particular transaction may not involve them in a credit loss; but by paying them less than the risk justifies, it undermines their ability to meet their losses elsewhere. It is easy to belittle this in an individual case, but the cumulative impact of this type of mistake can undermine a bank's profitability, and even its long-term viability.

For these reasons it is important that banks focus on all types of risk, and on their new and changing relationships to each other. Only in that way will they organize themselves appropriately to meet the changing market, and avoid major losses while trying to find and staff the new pattern of organization.

THE PURPOSE AND STRUCTURE OF THE BOOK

The author of this book is a credit specialist, who has been making credit decisions in relation to many of the new products. He has also been involved in discussions in his own bank on the theoretical basis for assessing the risks, and on the best organization to handle credit in the current environment.

This experience suggests a need to set out in detail the various types of risk banks are running, and how to recognize them; also, as part of this exercise, and as a useful exercise in its own right, to discuss various instruments and show how the different categories of risk appear and intermingle in each of them. The book does not aim to be a catalogue of all instruments; they are appearing and disappearing so fast that this would be a futile attempt, even if it had intrinsic value. Rather the aim is to give examples and to help bankers to build a framework of thought which they can then apply to each new instrument or variant as it raises its head. Learning by rote is neither practical nor desirable; a framework for constructive and imaginative thought is both.

The book is written from the viewpoint of a credit specialist, but because it recognizes the interaction of other risks with credit it spends much time on non-credit risks. The approach is not mathematical; although there are sections on exposure, to which a mathematical approach can apply, the book is concerned with the factors which lie behind the need to make judgements, not with mathematical representations. However valuable these may be in some areas, they only obscure the need for calm thought, common sense and judgement in assessing credit risk. The book does not deal with the risks of fraud; while important these are a separate subject.

The book falls into four parts. The first is something of an overview of the broad categories of risk, and how they relate to each other and the borrower/counterparty. The second is a much more detailed discussion of each of the various categories of risk, and the numerous subcategories. The third describes the major instruments now in common use and the risks which each attracts. And the fourth discusses the need for capital which each risk carries, the need for remuneration related to both the risk and the capital, the reaction of regulators and how these in turn affect the banks.

Each chapter has a brief glossary at the beginning, covering words and phrases which are important in the chapter. A word or phrase will not always be in the glossary of the chapter in which it first appears. A list of glossary items appears at the beginning of the book, which shows where each item in the glossary can be found.

Part I

Recognizing Risk

2 The Different Types of Risk

GLOSSARY

Contracts for differences Arrangements where counterparties agree to fix a future price now, and pay it regardless of the actual price when the date comes. A bank, for instance, might enter into a forward exchange contract fixing a price of £1·00 to $2·00 six months hence. If in six months the actual rate is £1·00 to $1·80, the bank gains or loses, depending on which side it was, by the amount of the difference. Alternatively, the client buys protection against the differences.

Exposure The maximum credit loss on a transaction, or group of transactions, on the worst possible assumptions. For a loan, this is the face amount of the loan. The concept involves no view of the probability that the worst will happen, merely identifies it.

LIBID London interbank bid rate, or the rate banks bid for deposits in the London interbank market.

LIBOR London interbank offered rate or the rate at which banks offer to lend in the London interbank market.

LIMEAN The mean of LIBOR and LIBID.

(Similar definitions can be derived by changing the first letter to denote a different centre. Thus PIBOR is Paris offered rate, FIBID Frankfurt bid rate, and so on.)

Risk The probability of loss. While exposure is a fact, or at worst a matter of calculation, risk is a matter of judgement.

Settlement risk The risk of loss in settling a two-way transaction. One side may perform and the other not; the performing side then risks the full amount it pays or value of what it delivers. Or the failure is known in time to avoid this risk but still leaves the need to replace the missing item at a price which may have changed.

Trading risk The risk of loss from a move in prices of securities or money market instruments, in interest rates or exchange rates, or in prices of bullion or financial or real assets.

Underwriting risk The risk of undertaking to buy securities or other financial assets at original issue at a fixed price or yield without the certainty that they can be resold at a profit – or sometimes at all.

Traditional security underwriting risk is short-term, but some of the newer forms of underwriting (NIFs, for instance) may be medium- or even long-term.

RISK *v.* EXPOSURE

Banks are, importantly, managers of risk. They justify their existence by taking risks which others are not prepared, or are less well qualified, to take, and making a profit from so doing. There is more to banking than risk management, of course, but this is at its heart. And although the types of risks banks take are changing, the essential art of banking, to be paid for taking well-judged risks, remains.

Banks must manage risk to minimize the actual losses arising from them, and to maximize the earnings they receive. Judging risk accurately is as important to maximize earnings as it is to minimize loss. A bank which underestimates the risks it takes will lose more than it should, but will also consistently charge less than it should, and often than it could. Equally, however, a bank which over-estimates risk will charge too much, and lose business to other banks, thus reducing its income. It is one thing to lose business where another bank has underestimated the risk; quite another when the other bank's view is correct.

The amount a bank can expect to lose on its total portfolio is a factor of the size of the portfolio and the risk attached to each part of it, modified by the skill with which the bank manages its risks and uses the various protections open to it. Put another way, the likely credit loss is a factor of credit risk related to total exposure. The same is true, *pari passu*, when looking at the bank's chances of loss from a single borrower; or from an activity giving rise to similar types of exposure from many borrowers or counterparties (securities settlement, for instance).

The distinction is important, because some activities give rise to large exposures with low risk; others to smaller exposures with higher risk. In some cases the risk of any loss may be low, but the chances are that if there is a loss it will be all or most of the exposure. In others the chance of some loss may be higher, but the chance of losing the whole amount much less. And in yet others the chance of loss may be small, and the chance of losing the whole exposure only a fraction of that.

The judgement as to whether a transaction represents an acceptable risk for a bank is thus based on both exposure and risk. If a bank accepts an exposure of half its net worth, failure will be catastrophic. Banks do accept exposures of that size (although rarely loan exposures); but they normally, rightly, require a very senior official to approve them. He in turn will want to be sure not only that the risk of any loss is low, but also that the risk of total loss is negligible.

Exposure is thus often the basis on which banks decide who can approve credit risks of a given size. It is also the accounting mechanism by which banks report to their shareholders. In traditional commercial banking it is quite simply the size of their assets plus, in the case of unused facilities, the assets they would hold if all facilities were fully used. (The exposure on an unused facility is the same as if it were fully used; the worst that can happen is that the borrower uses it fully and then fails.)

The distinction between risk and exposure is thus at the heart of risk management. Without systems which properly identify exposure, management does not know the total amounts it has at risk, nor individual bankers the impact of their decisions. Even apart from accounting and reporting, it is important to know what is the worst that can happen. However unlikely it is, that worst defines the risk to the bank's future. Exposure, to an individual borrower or to a group of related risks, which is a large fraction of the bank's net worth and earnings has a different impact on the bank's future than a small percentage. Loss of the whole amount may undermine the bank's viability; even the threat of loss may cause rating agencies to downgrade a bank's debt, which can add substantially to the cost of funding and undermine its profits.

PROXIES FOR EXPOSURE

One feature of the whole trend to securitization, broadly defined, has been the breakdown of the clear distinction between risk and exposure. In particular, products such as swaps do not have a readily calculable exposure. The worst that can happen in the worst possible case is no longer the loss of a clearly defined asset. It is instead the loss arising, after a credit failure, from adverse movements in interest or exchange rates – or both. There may be no loss if rates move favourably; we can discount this possibility as being clearly not the worst that can happen. The question of what is the worst is much more difficult.

Take an interest rate swap as an example: an agreement whereby counterparties exchange streams of interest payments, based on a notional principal sum which does not itself change hands. Usually one party pays a fixed rate, the other a floating rate such as six-month LIBOR. The fixed rate payer will suffer if interest rates rise, and its counterparty fails. It will have to pay a higher fixed rate to continue to receive the same floating rate. On the other hand, the fixed rate receiver will lose if interest rates fall and its counterparty fails; it will receive a lower rate in return for paying the same floating rate. Or, in either case, the sound party may accept the risk against which the lost swap protected, and not replace it.

In neither case however do the counterparties know what will happen to interest rates, or when the failure (which is not expected at all) will happen if it does. With short-dated swaps, say under one year, there may be a practical limit to how far interest rates can move, but this really does not apply to longer-dated ones. Swaps are mostly in the five to ten year range, but a growing number go beyond ten years and a few beyond twenty. There is no theoretical limit to how far interest rates can move in such periods.

After some rather simple approaches in the early days of swaps, banks mostly seem to calculate exposure as the cost of replacing the failed swap with a new one. This still requires assumptions about the interest rates, however, which will be discussed in more detail in Chapter 7. Any formula will make assumptions about the worst reasonable cost. In most cases these assumptions will prove conservative; when applied to a bank's whole portfolio they should be as accurate as anything of this sort can be. This may not be true for specific swaps or single counterparties with several swaps taking similar positions, however. Since the proxies for exposure are based on the worst reasonable, rather than the worst possible case, the actual amount lost may sometimes be greater than the proxy suggests.

Bankers often assume that these contracts for differences, as they are sometimes called, carry less exposure than those for a loan. Usually they do, but not always. In those few cases where the exposure is greater in the swap it is important to understand this and to know why. In brief, both exposure and risk are concepts which are vital to the management of risk and of the risk/reward ratio. Banks which mismanage this relationship end up taking risks they should not take, or taking sound risks at an inadequate return, or a mixture of both.

BROAD CATEGORIES OF RISK

The purpose of this section is only to introduce the categories of risk; Chapters 4 and 5 will go into more detail as to the implications, nuances and subcategories. But throughout their business, banks need to put the risks into balance and perspective.

Credit risk

Credit risk, as defined in the glossary, normally arises directly from the status of the borrower/counterparty, but can be made greater or less by the nature of the transaction. A long-term loan carries more credit risk than a short-term one, for instance, because more companies fail in ten years than in one; or an unsecured loan carries more than a secured one to the same borrower, because secured lenders have the benefit of their security while unsecured lenders may recover nothing. Occasionally, with non-recourse financing, or loans which rely mainly on security, credit risk may depend so heavily on the transaction that there is no real borrowing entity.

Credit risk is important, and obvious, in straightforward loans. It is equally important in lending instruments such as bonds, FRNs or commercial paper, but may be overlooked; these also carry a trading, and sometimes underwriting, risk which may be greater in the short term. In trading instruments, such as forward exchange and swaps, the trading risk may be pre-eminent; even where it is not these instruments are created mainly by traders, who see, and are expert in, trading risk but may either not recognize credit risk at all, or underestimate its importance. Credit risk also appears in various types of settlement risk, can be created by errors in documentation or operations, and is all-pervading in the work of a commercial bank.

Trading risk

Trading risk was historically quite separate from credit risk. The funding of bank loans often came mainly from current account deposits, or from deposits where interest was linked to a rate (such as Bank rate and more recently Base Rate in the United Kingdom) which was also used to set the cost of most borrowing. Even with the development of interbank markets and loans linked to them, the need to trade in deposits was kept separate from the credit risk; the assumption on which the bank priced such loans was that Treasury would immediately fund at LIBOR (or PIBOR, FIBOR and so on, depending on the financial centre). Thus the margin over LIBOR described the bank's profit from lending. If Treasury chose to fund in some other way for an additional profit, that was their business and entirely separate from the decision to lend at a particular margin. When this assumption was first made it was valid, but conditions have changed.

Banks, or at least the stronger ones, can now raise money at LIBID or below, while other types of borrowing offer, at least to the best corporate credits, short-term funds at LIMEAN, LIBID or lower. Depending on the exact reaction of management in each case, banks now face either lending at rates which on the old criteria give an inadequate return, or relying on their traders to get an extra return which compensates for both trading and credit risk, or letting their traders go out and find their own assets, rather than rely on the banking side to do so. Most banks combine all three, though with varying weights. In addition, there is a growing trade in loan sales. Some banks are more inclined to lend at low rates because they can sell the loan at a profit, taking it off balance sheet and reducing the related credit risk and the need for capital. Some, indeed, make a business out of lending in order to sell. Equally there would be no market for such loan sales if some, mostly smaller, banks were not eager to buy rather than generate their own. For some this is the only way to get access to high quality loan assets. But in each case the division between credit risk and trading risk is undermined. When a lender decides what to approve, he must be aware of the nature of the trading risks, and of how a credit risk which went wrong could affect them. And a trader must learn that taking the asset with the highest return, or best trading characteristic, may mean taking a higher credit risk than he recognizes or than the bank wants.

The same basic point applies to loan substitutes such as commercial paper and FRNs. But these introduce a new factor. The credit judgement must include a qualitative assessment, not just pass or fail. Otherwise the trader will take the higher yield, which will usually mean the higher risk; even though the absolute risk may be acceptable at a price in either case, a bank should not prefer medium-rated paper to high-rated at the same yield.

Similar points apply to instruments such as swaps, forward exchange deals, options, caps, futures and so on. In each case the trading risk needs to be clear to the lender who approves the credit; the credit risk must also be clear to the trader if he is to give the credit man the necessary information. There is no suggestion that credit men should make trading judgements, or traders credit judgements; only that each needs to know more about the other's field than he used to, to make the best decisions in his own field.

Underwriting risk

Here again the nature of underwriting risk is changing, and becoming more involved with credit risk. In its original meaning (other than in insurance which this book does not cover), underwriters took a rather extreme version of a short-term trading risk. In effect they bought a large trading position for immediate resale. How far they could subunderwrite the risk, and for how long they committed before they could sell, varied from market to market. The trading risk was extreme because the whole issue had to be sold at once; because there was usually some delay between their commitment to a specific price and sale, so that the market might move; and because the issue was new, with no established market against which to judge the reception (except for secondary issues). Nevertheless the period was always short; the risk was usually small; and even where the underwriters were caught, the loss from later sale at a lower price was a small percentage of the issue's face value.

There was always an element of credit risk, at least in underwriting debt; but it was more one of judging the market's perception of the credit than a direct risk. If the underwriter assessed the credit risk as lower than the market did, it would price the issue too high and perhaps have to reduce its price, and sell at a loss. Some credits are vulnerable to specific events (such as a change in the price of a key raw material, or protectionism in a major market). The underwriter could lose if one of these occurred between his pricing the deal and selling the issue. But actual loss due to bankruptcy, rather than to the more or less distant threat of it, should not be an issue in securities underwriting.

More recently, however, underwriting has crept into commercial banking and into the hybrid products that have elements of commercial and investment banking in them. Underwriting first entered commercial banking in a major way through the syndicated loan. Competition made banks take larger commitments than they really wanted to keep. It became common therefore for one or a small group of banks to commit to lend the whole of a very large facility, with a view to syndicating it and 'selling down' to the level they wanted to keep. Anything they could not sell down they would lend themselves. Usually syndication took place before the signing of the loan agreement, so that the non-underwriting banks came in as direct lenders; occasionally the underwriter signed up for the whole amount, and participated the loan out afterwards. In the then state of the law and market, however, the first method was much the sounder.

The syndicated loan underwriter accepted greater and different risks than the securities underwriter in several ways. First, the underwriting period was longer; depending on the circumstances, it might be weeks or months, rather than days, before he knew that he had successfully sold down, and sometimes even longer before the agreement was signed, and the sale irrevocable. Secondly, if he failed to sell down he had, until the early 1980s, an almost completely unmarketable asset. More recently loans have become more marketable, and various devices have tried to make them even more so; nevertheless a loan is always less liquid than a security quoted on an exchange. The NIF, RUF concept introduced even more risk to underwriting; indeed, while it is called underwriting, this may be a misnomer. Whereas the glossary definition refers to committing to purchase with a view to resale, underwriters of a NIF commit to purchase at a low margin in case of failure to sell, either at all, or below a tight price. (The instrument they commit to purchase is often different from the one that they or another bank have failed to sell, but the issuer and underlying credit risk are the same). Furthermore the risk in underwriting a NIF is always intended to last the whole life of the facility; a normal underwriting risk is intended to be short-term and only becomes long-term if the original assessment of the risk proves wrong. Probably a better way of looking at it is as a commitment to lend, knowing that the commitment will only be called in adverse conditions.

Settlement risk

Settlement risk is not new; it has always existed for commercial banks in the foreign exchange business, and for investment banks and their clients or counterparties in settling securities purchases and sales. The most notorious example of settlement risk was the Herrstatt case in 1974. The German authorities closed a bank after business hours in Frankfurt, but before New York's close. Several banks which had done spot exchange deals with Herrstatt paid the DM but did not receive dollars. In this case the bank had the dollars and only the closure prevented payment; in other cases it might not have had them. The German authorities were heavily criticized for their precipitate action. The case illustrates how settlement risk expands where the two ends of the settlement are in different centres, with differing laws and regulatory practices; a wide discrepancy in time zones makes the problem even trickier.

Even where there is no physical split of this sort settlement risk needs careful assessment. There are many different settlement systems, with many degrees of delay, collateral value or lack of it and protection. With the opening of domestic markets to foreigners, some of the basic assumptions are being questioned. Some of them rested on membership of an exclusive club. The new members are often unwilling to accept the standing of members as proof of creditworthiness; in turn the old members may find the new less acceptable than those with whom they have dealt for many years. Even where there is no outright distrust, new members will ask questions about the rules, which may show up anomalies. And massive increases in volumes can put strains on even well-tried systems, let alone those that were designed before the advent of the computer.

As a result, the markets are becoming conscious of settlement risk in a way they did not need to be before. Up to a point this is wholly good; anything which makes people look at and understand risk better helps to reduce it, and may in the process improve efficiency in other ways as well. There is a point, however, beyond which consciousness of risk, without full understanding, can become counterproductive. The risk in settling any given transaction is both small and short-term; in some cases protection is so good that the risk is *de minimis*. However, since most settlement risks are both repetitive and cumulative, it is not enough to assess the risk on one day, and say that it is a sound short-term risk. The continuing operation means that while each risk is short-term, the bank faces that risk over the medium to long-term, and can lose money because of events which occur after the original judgement on the risk.

The risk is cumulative in two ways. First, it may be two, three or more days before a bank knows whether its counterparty has settled. If in the meantime it continues to deal, it may be at risk for several days' transactions, not just one. Or it may deal with the same or closely related counterparties in several different markets, say in the London gilt and equity markets, in Paris, Frankfurt and the eurobond market. It might easily deal through different units each of which controlled the risk they were taking. However, if the counterparty defaulted, the bank would face loss on the unsettled transactions in all centres. The need to centralize control, or at least recording, of all counterparty exposures is one of the hardest decisions banks face today. Failure to do so could leave them more exposed than is prudent ('could', but it is hard to tell whether it would). Yet the cost of doing it, in cash and bureaucratic procedures, could be prohibitive. Unless all banks decide the same way, and control their costs with similar skill, some are going to suffer.

One method of reducing settlement risk is a clearing house of some sort. However the users then have a risk on the clearing house if it fails to clear properly; or members of the clearing house may find themselves liable for the loss to others where the clearing house fails.

Documentation risk

The increase in the length, complexity and cost of documentation since the early 1960s in part reflects the underlying increase in the complexity of products; in part the need to cover more possible causes of loss as a result of experience; in part the growing dominance of lawyers as banks step into new fields with unknown minefields in them.

Unfortunately lawyers, with a few honourable exceptions, think only of what happens when (again only the best think of it as 'if') the agreement gets into court. Important though this is, the need to write for judges obscures the need to write for the people who will use all agreements throughout their life; the clerks in the operating/financial divisions of the banks and their counterparties. If they misunderstand the document, or if it does not work because the lawyers have not understood the transaction, a loss is much more likely than because a court interprets the agreement in a way which surprises one party. Bankers are also at fault, but ultimately the lawyers draft documents, not bankers.

This risk may be partly offset by a market tendency to standardize clauses. Once a particular phrasing becomes widely known, it is less likely to be misunderstood. This has been carried a stage further in the case of swaps, where ISDA (the International Swap Dealers' Association) in New York and the British Bankers Association (BBA) in London have moved towards standardizing documentation. Their approaches have been rather different, and ISDA's has been the more comprehensive. It is unfortunate that there are now two standards instead of one; ISDA's, while excellent in concept, has been drafted in a way which is hard to understand.

The other risk in standardization, particularly internationally, is that it takes some time before the various points are tested in court. If they fail the test, there are numerous agreements caught by the failure, with little chance of pleading different facts. If the assumptions behind the ISDA agreement, for instance, prove to be wrong, or to be correct under US law but not under French law, there will be red faces, and losses.

Operating risk

Operating risk arises from a mixture of the complexity, novelty, volume and lack of uniformity of the transactions; lack of clarity in drafting; poor understanding of the deal and of operating restraints shown in drafting; the control by the banker of the wilder fancies of both lawyer and client; it is offset in part by the quality of the systems and of the people operating them and their training.

It is not too difficult to see that complex transactions are more likely to cause operating errors, and risk of operating loss, than simple ones. It is easy for both client and banker to forget that the sophisticated variations to standard facilities (often referred to as 'bells and whistles') almost always complicate them. Whether the added value justifies the complication needs more thought than it often gets.

Novelty, too, can cause operating errors, and the more numerous the novelties, and the more complex, the greater the risk of a mistake by someone not yet familiar with all the ramifications. Again, the introduction of novelties as a marketing ploy, rather than because they add real value, is often a source of unnecessary risk.

Volume of work, and particularly rapid increases in volume at short notice, put a strain on the people handling them that is bound to cause mistakes. When the volume increase includes a large share of complicated novelties the number of mistakes inevitably grows. Not all mistakes lead to significant loss, but the more mistakes there are, the greater the chance that some will prove expensive.

As the previous section suggested, even fairly simple transactions can be made to seem complex by legal drafting. To be fair this is not all the fault of the lawyers. Regulators and legislators can threaten banks with so many penalties that the lawyers rightly draft protective wording; or the courts can rule on a transaction in a way that has implications for many other transactions, which the lawyers then need to deal with. None of this is an argument against careful drafting, legislation or regulation; it is a plea to all concerned to remember that complication equals risk, and unnecessary complication equals unnecessary risk. Wording or regulations intended to protect against a minor risk may create a more serious one. This should be of most concern to lawyers representing banks, and to prudential regulators. Even regulators such as the Securities Exchange Commission (SEC) or the Securities Industry Board (SIB) whose main concern is with protecting the clients rather than the industry should remember that obscure wording to meet their requirements probably confuses rather than helps the client.

A bank can guard against the worst operating risks by having sound operating systems, high quality people with continuity of experience in their jobs, and first class training and controls. Even this cannot guarantee against operating loss, but makes it less likely to be lethal. Unfortunately conditions which create the worst operating risks also make it harder to install these protections. Novelties are hard to fit into even the most flexible computer-based systems; volume puts a strain onto systems as well as people; complexity also is difficult to fit into systems; the combination of complexity and innovation often means that too many transactions have to be handled as manual exceptions; and dealing with crises caused by too much complexity and surges in volume makes it difficult to spend much time on training.

The settlement problems of London brokers after Big Bang provide one, highly publicized, example of this type of cumulative operating risk.

On and off balance sheet risk

The sense of the phrase 'off balance sheet risk' has changed. Originally it referred to risk – and in banking terms the finance which went with the risk – which was isolated from the main business of a company. Then, if the off balance sheet risk proved unsound, the repercussions were confined to the particular project. True non-recourse project finance carries no financial risk for companies operating the project, other than their original investment. Hence the risk was properly 'off balance sheet' since only profits could come on balance sheet. Purists would claim that this is still the only correct usage.

More recently, however, the phrase has been narrowed to mean risks which do not show on the face of the balance sheet; in some countries they may be footnoted, others do not even require a footnote. There can be genuine reasons for not showing them; a forward exchange contract is hard to quantify and is in any case more like a contra item than a true balance sheet item. Often, though, off balance sheet items are used as a form of window dressing; companies hope that banks, shareholders and perhaps even rating agencies will fail to notice the risk, or in items like leasing the actual obligation; banks hope the regulators – and again rating agencies – will not require the same level of capital to support off balance sheet risks as they do those on balance sheet. The phrase thus includes instruments where the accountants have misunderstood the risk, such as partial recourse facilities; unused commitments and guarantees which can turn into full-blown loan exposure; forward exchange and swaps where only a small part of the face value may come on balance sheet, and then only in a worst-case scenario.

Regulators and accountants in various countries look on the subject from different angles and with different degrees of severity. In the banking field this threatens to give banks from laxer countries a competitive advantage, leading to calls for 'level playing fields'. The whole question of off balance sheet risk has thus become a major concern for regulators in international banking and even has political repercussions.

Levels of seniority

Although the main risks in banking relate to the borrower or the transaction, banks need to know the relative seniority of their debt. Whether or not a particular debt is senior or junior will not affect the chances that the borrower will fail (although the overall mix of debt in a borrower's balance sheet may). It will, however, severely affect the size of recovery in case of trouble. Broadly speaking, in liquidation any given level of seniority will be paid in full before the next level receives anything.

This is crucial, because a bank should not expect to lose the whole loan even if a borrower fails. Either it should be a senior lender, or it should ensure that all lenders are equal. In this way, the bank almost always recovers at least something from the company's assets; often, it recovers over 50 per cent. If it allows itself to be junior to other lenders, however, this is much less likely to be true. This will change the number of cases where it makes a loss only marginally; the average size of those losses will be greater.

In this context, equity is the most junior; although there are rankings within equity, all of them are junior to any form of debt. Their compensation, at least for ordinary or common shares, is to receive directly or through growth in the share price all the profits of a successful enterprise. Hence the phrase 'equity risk', at least as used by commercial bankers, has two implications. It is a level of risk which no bank should take; conversely, anyone who does take it, including an unwilling lender, deserves a share of the profits.

Political risk

Political risk has many ramifications which are discussed in detail in the author's *Lending in International Commercial Banking* (second edition, Macmillan, 1988). For the purposes of this book the most important aspects of risk are not those which directly relate to the credit of a borrower, but rather those which can affect whole classes of a bank's operation: the developments in regulation of both commercial and investment banking, particularly the joint proposals of the Bank of England and Federal Reserve on capital adequacy, leading on to those of the Basle Committee; everything attached to Big Bang in Britain, and similar if less dramatic developments in many other countries; changes in the past years in insolvency laws in Britain and the United States and the prospect of similar – or perhaps dissimilar – changes in other countries; legal interpretations which change longstanding views on security or other key aspects of credit (such as the Charge Card case (1986) in Britain which undermined the traditional basis for lending against cash collateral); the worry about how courts in different countries will interpret the legal drafting of new products – and about what will happen if different countries interpret the same product differently; and perhaps above all the worry as to how much further the various forms of deregulation will go and whether and if so how far the pendulum will swing back.

Another aspect of political risk that is changing is what might be called reverse political risk. Many bankers have argued over the years that the government would not allow such and such a company to fail for political rather than commercial reasons. Until the early 1980s they seemed broadly right, although many bankers remained wary of what seemed to them a thin basis for credit judgement. During the

1980s this concern has been justified. There seem to be two main reasons for this; one is the growing tendency of even nominally left wing governments to put more trust in the power of the market, and therefore to be unwilling to bail out lame ducks which a few years previously they would have rescued as a matter of course. The second, which may have played a part in causing the first, was that so many countries ran out of borrowing capacity, often partly owing to the cost of propping up sick companies. The question ceased to be 'would' or 'should' a government rescue each ailing company, but 'could' it? Even countries which had not reached this stage began to worry that they might do so.

In brief banks need to worry about the legal, regulatory and political climate internationally and in each country in which they do business. Not only is the banking business changing so fast that there is little precedent to guide us in many cases, but the background is also changing; this further reduces banks' ability to assess the impact of the changes they generate.

HOW RISKS INTERACT

Risks in banking have always interacted to some extent, but the linkage has grown and become more complex in the 1980s. There are several different types. One is the way in which some of the other types of risk can affect the level of credit risk. For example, swaps can either improve or weaken the credit of a borrower. Any improvement in most cases will be marginal, but the weakening may be more serious. The improvement arises when companies use swaps to protect themselves against risk; an interest rate swap, for instance, may reduce a company's exposure to rising rates, or a currency swap to exchange volatility. However this assumes that the company uses swaps to hedge only; if it decides to speculate in swaps it can lose as much money as when speculating in commodities or other high-risk instruments.

Equally credit risk can create a trading position, or expose a company to a trading risk opposite to the one it thought it had. A bank may carefully match two swaps, so that in one it pays fixed and in the other it receives it, with a margin. If one of the counterparties fails, the bank no longer has a matched position, but a trading risk on the resulting open position. Or if the bank used a swap to take a long position in fixed rate, a failed counterparty leaves it short.

Credit risk and documentation risk also interact. If a credit is sound, it is less likely that the borrower will test the document in court. While there can be differences of opinion about what a document meant even between a bank and a sound credit, they usually reach agreement amicably. Where a company is in trouble, however, the exact interpretation of the bank's rights to accelerate, of the ranking of debt and of the validity of security becomes crucial. At the same time a liquidator or administrator, or the local equivalent, will scrutinize the bank's documentation much more closely than do most managements.

Political, credit and documentation risk are all mixed up together, too. A sound credit will not argue theological points in documentation; sound drafting will not give the opportunity; a sound legal system will not give the incentive. But legislation must be interpreted by the courts, and if the law is unclear or the courts unused to commercial, and particularly to international, practice the combination may be lethal. Some court systems are corrupt, some are politically motivated and some are basically incompetent. Some are perfectly sound but take an idiosyncratic view of particular items. All of these risks need to be recognized as part of the credit decisions, but banks or their lawyers also need to know whether there are ways to avoid them. The greater the political risk, whether documentary or otherwise, the better the credit needs to be to justify the view that political risk cannot be critical to recovery of the bank's funds.

In one sense settlement risk is credit risk. If the counterparty meets its side of the bargain, the other risks are academic; they become real only if the credit risk turns sour. But there are two types of settlement risk. One is the risk of outright loss resulting from a payment which is not met by delivery; the other is the market risk of fluctuation when the counterparty fails to deliver and the price of what it was to deliver changes before the bank can buy it in. Of course the two can combine, but again they are intertwined and to some extent contingent.

Operations risk also intertwines with credit risk. A failure to collect money when due, for instance, increases the risk that the borrower will spend it elsewhere and be unable to pay it when the bank finally claims it. A failure to enforce the conditions of the agreement as to collateral, information, ratio covenants and so on may act as a constructive waiver. Then when the clauses are needed the courts will not enforce them.

There are other ways in which risks are intertwined or at least affect each other but this section does not aim to catalogue them, just to highlight the point.

3 Understanding the Risk

GLOSSARY

Cash flow Net profit after taxes, plus depreciation, plus or minus other non-cash charges or credits. This measures the actual cash generated from operations after adjusting for accrual accounting, and thus a company's ability to produce enough cash to meet its obligations. The phrase is also used more loosely to mean the cash available for debt service after meeting essential requirements such as capital expenditure and net working investment. In this context a reduction in net working investment is an addition to cash flow. The phrase is also used in the plural in relation to the actual cash payments of a continuing transaction, such as a swap.

Net working investment The portion of current assets directly related to volume of business, and which cannot be financed by current liabilities equally so related. For most companies this means receivables plus inventory minus payables; where companies receive advance payments, or borrow on a purely self liquidating basis, the figure may be adjusted to take account of this. One value is to allow forecasts of the additional borrowing related to a given increase in volume.

Seniority The order in which debt will be paid in liquidation. Secured debt is the most senior if the security meets the whole claim; any shortfall ranks as ordinary unsecured debt. Most unsecured debt ranks equally, but in some countries, Spain for example, there may be complicated rankings within unsecured debt. Subordinated debt ranks below senior debt but may have rankings within itself.

Subordinated debt Where the lender contracts that his debt will rank behind some or all other debt in liquidation; some subordinated debt also restricts payment of interest or principal even short of liquidation. Because the concept is contractual the exact details depend on the contract.

Zero sum A transaction or series of transactions which give rise to neither profit nor loss overall; that is, one party can make a profit only if another makes a loss.

THE STRENGTH OF THE BORROWER

In looking at credit risk, banks look first at the strength of the borrower/counterparty, except in the few cases of a pure transaction or asset risk. The analytical approach to assessing this strength is covered in full in T. H. Donaldson, *Understanding Corporate Credit* (Macmillan, 1984).

A company has, or lacks, some combination of balance sheet strength and earning capacity; more particularly the ability to generate cash from operations faster than is needed just to keep the company running and competitive.

For most manufacturing and commercial companies cash flow is the key to credit standing. Balance sheet strength provides a second line of support, while a weak balance sheet may absorb cash flow that the company needs to keep its operations sound. In other words, cash flow analysis has to look at a company's need for cash as well as its ability to generate it and ensure that the two are in balance. Since credit is about risk, analysis must assess all the factors which might change either the components or the balance itself. Apart from operating/commercial risks particular to each company's business there are financial risks. These may relate to the balance sheet structure in general, or to specific items. These include exposure to fluctuations in interest and exchange rates.

The same basic points are true of asset-based companies, such as leasing or commodity companies, except that here we are looking to assets to repay the debt: assets realized in the normal course of business, however, not in liquidation or in a way which damages the company's viability. Even in asset-based companies we look for some profits, to pay interest even where assets pay principal; and to provide the key to their value as well as to the health of the business.

Where the borrower/counterparty is not a company, we can apply different analytical techniques, depending on its exact nature. For a country or its agency the analysis relates to political and social stability, economic and human resources, financial capacity and so on. See *Lending in International Commercial Banking* for a fuller discussion.

Whatever the exact nature of the borrower/counterparty, in most cases its strength or weakness will decide the credit risk. Whatever the nature of the transaction, even when there is no direct recourse, the bank needs to be sure that the borrower will meet its obligations. On the other hand the nature of the transaction affects the credit risk in two ways. It may strengthen or weaken the credit or it may make the loss greater or less if the credit turns sour.

DOES THE TRANSACTION CHANGE THE CREDIT OF THE BORROWER?

In one sense, any transaction can change a company's credit standing; whether the change is for better or worse depends on the circumstances as well as the transaction. Take, for example, a medium-term fixed rate loan. Where this funds short-term floating rate debt, it usually improves the credit; at the very least it provides certainty as to the interest payable. If the fixed rate is moderate, and floating rates seem about to rise sharply, it may avoid a large increase in cost and decline in profit. If however, the fixed rate is high, and floating rates seem likely to fall, it may weaken the credit, although even here certainty is worth something. If the company already has predominantly fixed rate debt, it may further unbalance the financial structure. Net new debt, rather than refunding, weakens the credit unless it is used to create an offsetting strength.

Other transactions can have similar or contrary effects, depending on the circumstances. For instance, a forward exchange contract can strengthen the credit of a major importer or exporter. The former may be heavily at risk if the currency in which it is invoiced strengthens rapidly; the latter from a weakening of the foreign currency in which it sells. The risk, and protection, is even greater where the company borrows foreign currency for domestic use.

However, ill-advised forward exchange business can weaken a company. To hedge against the risk of a currency moving in one direction protects against loss but also precludes any profit from moves in the opposite direction. Generally speaking, the hedge against loss is more important than the lost profit. With a hedged exchange risk, whatever the form of the hedge, the company knows what its cost or income will be and can adjust the rest of its costs or prices to ensure a profit. The risk of speculative losses hurts credit standing more than the hope, or even reality, of speculative gains helps it. The profits, after all, will be recognized as low quality; the losses will be seen as the result of poor judgement which may raise wider questions about management.

Nevertheless there are cases where the trend of currencies is so clear, and the impact on prices so strong, that the only sound judgement is not to hedge. In these cases, a forward exchange contract or any other form of hedge can actually weaken credit.

Where a company is using forward exchange to cover open positions arising in the ordinary course of its business, the impact on its credit will usually be modest. Where a company is in difficulties for other reasons, uncovered forex positions may tip it over the edge, or a hedge may avoid this. But in most cases, the impact on overall profits and credit standing will be marginal. Even if the company hedges where there is no need and loses a profit opportunity, it should still make the profit on operations that the hedge was designed to protect. And while unhedged losses can push an unhealthy company over the brink, it is rarely currency risk that brings it to the brink in the first place. The few exceptions, such as contractors on long-term projects, have a clear incentive to hedge.

The risk to a company is much more serious where it is speculating in exchange to make a profit. There is a real danger that companies which need to do a volume exchange business begin to believe that the money they save is a sign of a natural ability. Some then begin to try to make profits from treasury operations in their own right, rather than merely protect the profits they expect to make in their normal business.

It is difficult to lose much money protecting assets, because the risk is of an opportunity loss related to the assets being protected. A speculative loss is a cash loss and has no natural size limit. Worst of all is a loss made trying to recover from an initial speculative loss.

Much the same is true of swaps. Properly used they can protect against loss on interest or currency movements. The approach is much the same as with foreign exchange or fixed rate borrowing, except that the term is longer than most forex transactions. Even where the usage is unskilful or unlucky, any loss on a genuine attempt to hedge is more likely to be an opportunity loss than a cash loss. But again, very large sums can be lost speculating in the swap market.

We could run through all the trading or hedging instruments in the market. A few will do little to change a company's strength. Most, however, will improve the credit where they are used skilfully to reduce the risk inherent in exposure to interest rate, exchange rate or commodity price fluctuations. Even where they are used unskilfully, the worst that can happen is usually a small opportunity loss. The profits or losses will rarely be significant in themselves, although they may tip the balance in a few troubled situations. Speculation, on the other hand, can, on its own, bring a company down. Even successful speculation weakens the bank's view of a company's credit; the earnings are low quality and the bank knows that the risks which create the profits could cause losses as large or larger next time.

In principle, bonds, FRNs and similar borrowing instruments

should have no more impact on a company's credit than a comparable bank loan. If it is sound to borrow at a floating rate for seven years from the banks, then a seven-year FRN should also be sound; similarly with a fixed rate bond, or even with a bond in a foreign currency. In most cases this basic principle is true in practice as well, although there are a few points which can change this. They will not do so on their own and only rarely even in combination with other factors; but because they are less obvious they are more likely to be overlooked than the traditional risks. They may tip the scales when they need not have done so. The risk arises from two factors that many borrowers see as an advantage. These are the wide spread of bondholders, and the frequent lack of full protective documentation. Neither of these can cause the initial weakness, but they can contribute to a failure to deal with it in the most effective way.

Creating a wide spread of ownership of the debt is seen as opening up new sources of funds to a company. This intensifies competition and reduces cost or makes available funds for a term or with other desirable features not on offer from the banks. All of which is perfectly true as far as it goes. However wider ownership dilutes loyalty and may put the company's future in the hands of 'Belgian dentists' who have no skill or interest in working with a troubled company to turn it around. This may be partly offset where the holders are largely institutions, or where there is a trustee who is both able and willing to play the role on behalf of the bondholders. These conditions exist in some domestic bond markets but are largely lacking in the eurobond markets. Many eurobonds have no trustee; even where there is one, eurobonds are bearer bonds. This makes it hard to develop a consensus to enable bondholders to act effectively.

Again, a prime advantage of a bond for many holders is liquidity. However one implication of liquidity is that the holder can run at the first sign of trouble. In practice of course even the most liquid instrument becomes virtually unsaleable once the issuer is known to be in trouble – or saleable only at a heavy loss. A holder for whom liquidity is a key virtue is not going to hold onto the bond to support rescue attempts. If he cannot sell, he will be looking for his money back as soon as he can get it; he will have neither the knowledge nor the patience to work through a restructuring. If he can sell, the buyer may be either someone who is a little less alert, but otherwise similar, or a professional arbitrageur, looking for a quick return, not a long-term relationship.

Equally, the lack of protective covenants required in most eurobond issues contrasts strongly with at least the better bank loans. Many companies resist covenants and regard their absence as a plus factor. But properly viewed and used covenants support a credit. We must be careful not to exaggerate their power or importance; if management is incompetent, or if conditions are so heavily against a company that no management can save it, the mere existence of covenants will not do so, nor insure the banks against loss. Then again, if management has its own, effective controls, it may argue that covenants add little. There are cases, however, where covenants provide a warning sign to management, or allow the lender to issue a warning which management heeds. Their absence therefore weakens a company's credit in those cases where a management could save the day, and an intelligent outsider causes an early move.

DOES THE TRANSACTION CHANGE THE PROBABLE SIZE OF LOSS?

Most assessments of credit relate to the prospect of failure. This is the most important aspect of credit; if the borrower/counterparty does not fail, there will be no loss for credit reasons although there may still be for other reasons.

But the success of credit control relates to more than the number of defaults; it also covers their cost. Even exposures which do not add to the risk of default can give rise to different levels of cost if the default happens anyway. Banks which consistently take risks which give rise to high losses may lose more money than banks with more defaults but a lower percentage loss on each one.

The most obvious example is loans of differing seniority. If one lender has a pledge over valuable assets, he may be paid out in full or nearly so; this payment may exhaust the main value of the bankrupt's assets so that other creditors receive little or nothing. The same is true of senior and subordinated debt. A borrower with realisable assets of £2 100 000, and preferred creditors of £100 000 would have assets of £2 million against liabilities of, say, £4 million. If all the creditors are on the same basis, each will receive 50 per cent of his claim. If £1 million of claims are secured on assets worth more than £1 million, they will be paid in full. The remaining £3 million of claims will now receive only 33·3 per cent of their face value. Conversely, if there is no secured claim but £1 million of claims are subordinated, the senior £3 million will receive 66·7 per cent of face value, while the subordinated receive nothing.

These legal rules also affect the negotiating position of the lenders in rescues short of full insolvency. In any form of reorganization, whether under insolvency laws or not, the party who would lose most from an insolvency will usually have to give up most to avoid it. On the other hand, a subordinated lender who gets little or nothing out of a restructuring proposal has no incentive to co-operate. He may therefore be able to negotiate a better deal than his legal position suggests. He cannot count on this in advance, since senior lenders will only agree if they still expect to recover more in a restructuring than in liquidation. A subordinated lender who is greedy or misjudges senior lenders' appetite for restructuring may overplay his hand.

There are other situations where the loss may be more or less than the face value of a loan. One example is secured debt where the security carries costs. A lender who arrests a ship, for instance, becomes liable for a wide range of costs, from flying the crew home to lay-up costs, insurance, maintenance and so on. If the ship realizes less than these costs the bank ends up losing more than if it had simply forgiven the debt. (This is not an academic point; banks have faced this situation often.)

Another example relates to a wide range of 'contracts for differences'. When a bank agrees an interest rate swap, for instance, there will be a notional principal value on which the interest streams are based. The amount at risk may be more or less than this notional principal. At the time the swap is agreed, neither party knows what such a loss might be. Indeed, if one party fails when interest rates are at the same level as at inception, there need be no loss. In many cases, any loss will be quite small, much less than the notional principal; the shorter the life of the swap, the more likely that any loss will be small. If the counterparty fails in the early days of the swap, interest rates probably have not moved far, keeping the cost of replacing the swap low. If the counterparty fails later in the life of the swap, the interest rate may have moved further, but there will be less remaining payments to replace. Equally the lower the starting interest rate, and the less volatile, the lower the likely loss.

Many interest rate swaps fit this pattern and the risk is a relatively small proportion of the notional principal. There is a danger that banks will assume too easily that all swaps are of lower risk than comparable loans. This is not the case. The longer the life of the swap, the higher the starting interest rate and the more volatile the rates involved, the greater the chance that the counterparty will fail when rates have moved heavily against the non-defaulter, but while there are still many payments due, which must be replaced at high cost. A twenty-year swap with a starting rate of ten per cent might fail after five years when interest rates had doubled. This leaves fifteen years at ten per cent to cover or, gross, 150 per cent of the notional principal. The exact replacement cost will depend on rate expectations and therefore the discount rate applied. However the same discount rate would apply in present valuing a loan, so that the relationship would remain the same. (This assumes that all payments are matched; where there is a sizeable mismatch the risk of loss it causes must be added to the rate risk, which can push the total well above the notional principal.) The same basic point is true of a cross-currency swap, except that here we have to take into account the possible movement in exchange rates and the repayment of principal. It is thus easier for a currency swap to cost more to replace than the notional principal with a shorter remaining life than fifteen years. The past and likely future volatility of the particular pair of exchange rates also affects the chances here.

The risk of loss on items such as options, futures, caps or collars can be assessed on a similar basis. Sometimes the risk is small, in others at least potentially much larger. The point though is that in each case the bank can assess whether the loss on default, on reasonable assumptions, is likely to be more than, less than or about the same as a loan. The decision to take the risk, and the amount to charge for taking it, require this assessment. Even sloppy procedures reach the correct answer some of the time, but banks should not rely on this.

Contracts for differences often carry settlement risk, and this may need to be added to the other risks described, or substituted for them. But settlement risk can also arise in buying and selling or even acting as custodian or agent. In guaranteed delivery versus payment (DVP) systems, the risk is only of a market loss where the counterparty fails to settle and the bank has to buy in. In some systems the process can take days or even weeks, but even so the maximum movement in the price should be only a fraction of the principal value. Where the system allows the payment to be made without receiving the security, or vice versa, the risk is the whole principal value, plus any adverse market movement.

The point, thus, is that the amount lost in case of default can vary widely, from a tiny fraction of the amount apparently at risk, to well over it. In deciding whether to take the risk, what to charge and whether to take extra protection, such as security, the bank needs to assess the amount it could lose in case of default, as well as the probability of default.

HAVE WE IDENTIFIED THE TRUE RISKS OF THE TRANSACTION?

The boom in securitization and in the range of new products, as well as the complex multi-product transactions, brings new risks. It also means that risks appear in different, almost disguised, forms. A crucial part of the decision to do a transaction therefore is an analysis of where the risk lies. In simple transactions, this analysis is also simple. For instance, sometimes a swap will call for one side to make a payment at the beginning, which will be offset over the life of the swap by lower interest payments. In swap terms this makes little difference; the different timing of the payments is discounted in calculating their exact size and if the swap runs its full course the end result is no different to a swap with fully matching payments. An experienced swap dealer might recognize that the upfront payment was more like a loan, and created an additional credit risk if the counterparty failed while a large part of it was still uncovered; and a credit man would be onto this point as soon as he understood the nature of the transaction. But a less experienced swap dealer would not look beyond the swap characteristics, and an inexperienced banker might never ask the questions which would show the extra credit risk.

There are many variants of the basic swap which do not change the swap characteristics but may change the credit risk or introduce new settlement or operating risks. Each swap which is in any way different from the basic fully matched swap needs to be reviewed by someone with knowledge of all types of risk. Only then can the bank be reasonably sure that nobody will say, too late: 'If I had known that was how it worked, I would never have approved it.'

In straightforward swaps, the hidden risks are mostly lightly camouflaged, and it takes only a modicum of common sense and probing to find them. Not all swaps are straightforward, however. The complications come in two broad ways. In one type, they are part of a series, either of swaps alone or of other transactions. A fairly simple example is of repackaged bonds, discussed in later chapters; a more complex example might revolve around a company's need for fixed rate debt where neither a bond issue nor private placement was appropriate. It might therefore need to borrow floating and swap into fixed. However, the need to draw down on an uncertain schedule, and to amortize over several years might preclude a straightforward swap. Instead the company might use a combination of caps, collars, forward swaps and ordinary swaps to give it the right mixture of flexibility and protection. If all the transactions were done with one bank, it would have a series of credit risks on that bank, which in turn would have a similar series with the counterparties with which it laid them off. If the bank merely acted as intermediary, the company might have credit risks on several different counterparties. It would have to consider the impact of the failure of each one before it could be sure whether the solution was as risk averse as, in swap terms, it seemed.

The second way is when swaps are used to create instruments which have some extra feature, or to eliminate some undesirable feature or even just to achieve the objective at lower cost. For instance, banks are always looking for ways to use caps and collars, alone or in conjunction with swaps, to provide instruments which are cheaper than swaps or protect against exposure in both directions or meet other needs.

Whatever the cause and nature of the complication, those analysing the risks, and assessing the bank's reward for taking them, must look at all the risks, not just those in their area of expertise.

Other areas where banks can underestimate the risks arise from securitization of debt. A trader in a bank's Treasury, for instance, may consider ECP and FRNs for the same issuer as largely interchangeable; they both call for a new rate to be reset periodically, and thus enable him to play the interest curve. From a credit point of view, however, ECP is a three- or six-month instrument with repayment at the end of the period. The decision whether to replace maturing ECP with new paper from the same issuer may often be taken without much thought; nevertheless it is a decision within the power of the bank, which has the opportunity to get out at each rollover. A bank needs sound systems to ensure that it gets out in time; this does not alter the point that it can do so.

FRNs, on the other hand, are bonds with a remaining life that may be as much as fifteen or twenty years and is frequently more than five. Although the interest is payable at the end of each period, the principal is not due until maturity. Of course the FRN is saleable, and some FRNs have genuinely liquid markets. Others either do not at all, or the liquidity is apt to dry up quickly when it is most needed.

Even the most liquid instrument can fluctuate in price; it will certainly do so if anything threatens its issuer's credit standing, and may do so for reasons which have nothing to do with the issuer's credit. There is thus a difference even in trading risk; FRNs are as good as ECP only while the market has no qualms about the longer term. With ECP, provided the credit risk has been correctly judged, the bank can get its money back in full and use it to take a different view; with an FRN this is not always true. Even the most liquid FRN may be saleable only at a loss, and less liquid ones may show a loss which the bank will not accept. As soon as that happens the apparent three- or six-month credit risk becomes longer-term. The market recognizes some of this extra risk in a higher yield for FRNs than for ECP, but it is not clear how to calculate the full risk.

FRNs may also be seen as loan substitutes, and are often referred to as such. The credit risk is seen as less than with a normal loan because of the liquidity. However, even if we ignore the doubts about liquidity already expressed, there are risks in buying FRNs rather than lending to the same borrower. One is the lack of a relationship and the consequent ability to follow the company's credit more closely. As already mentioned, eurobond documentation gives less protection and less ability to insist on corrective action. The lack of ratio covenants, and of a trustee, and the resulting doubts as to how the bond holders are to co-ordinate their position when a borrower proposes a restructuring; these are all as important in considering whether we have identified the true risks as whether the risks have changed.

In the early days of the eurobond market some of these points may have been largely academic; the investment banks persuaded issuers in trouble and their bank lenders that the payment of interest and principal on bonds was sacrosanct. The amount lent through bond issues was, at first, small enough for the banks to accept the loss involved to keep the borrower alive and thus improve the chances of recovering all or a large part of their debt. As bond issues became a larger part of the total debt, and the belief in recovery was eroded, banks became less willing to grant this preferred position. There are now many borrowers where bonds make up such a large part of their debt that they will not survive a problem unless bondholders take part in whatever support they need. The lack of tight documentation and a clear mechanism for representing the bondholders makes it hard to see how this will be achieved. This in turn introduces an element of risk into bonds, not only for their holders but for other lenders to borrowers which have large bond issues outstanding and run into trouble. It may prove even harder to carry subordinated bondholders in a restructuring.

One of the problems in all of these and many other types of risk is the absence of any standard basis for assessing the various risks. Even within each bank there will be differences of view as to how to assess their relationship; and a need to have everyone assess them on the same basis. Otherwise the bank itself will be preparing figures which treat apples and oranges alike; and what one bank calls oranges a second may call pears and a third bananas, making comparison between banks even harder than it now is.

There is thus a need to develop what some banks are beginning to call 'loan equivalents – or equivalence'. This is already showing up in the regulatory requirements for capital adequacy, and some banks are working on it internally, but the real need is for an industry-wide standard. This should not only apply to all existing facilities, but give clear guidelines which can be used to develop figures for new products as they appear. One day all bankers should be able to look at a product and say, 'That is equivalent to a one year unsecured loan of x'. They may not all reach the same value for x; the point is to use the same methodology so that the remaining differences reflect legitimate variations of professional judgement only. Until then we cannot really say that the recognition of credit risk, and of the extent of it in each type of transaction, is a science, or an art using scientific tools, rather than more or less intelligent guesswork. (Loan equivalents are discussed further in Chapter 8.)

RISK TRANSFERRED STILL EXISTS

Many of the new products are ways of transferring risk. It is easy to think that a risk transferred is a risk abolished; this is rarely so, for several reasons. A risk transferred may merely be transformed. For instance, a company which borrows at a floating rate and swaps into fixed changes one risk for two. First it changes the risk of cash loss if interest rates rise for that of opportunity loss if they fall. In many cases the latter is a more acceptable risk and the swapper is glad to have what it regards as the lesser risk; nevertheless risk remains. Secondly the swapper now has a credit risk; if its counterparty fails to perform, it will again be exposed to the risk it originally swapped to avoid.

In another sense the risk has not disappeared at all; it has merely been taken over by another party. Where a company swaps floating rate for fixed with a bank, the bank is then exposed to the floating rate risk – as well as the credit risk on the company. If the bank in turn lays off the swap risk with a third party, whether another bank or a client, this party then has the risk; the bank has a second credit risk. There is one exception to this; where the counterparties start with opposite risks, they may cancel out all except the credit risk. Thus to match a borrower vulnerable to rising rates with an investor exposed if rates fall leaves both free of trading risk; or at least of the risk which worries them. In practice banks rarely manage to match two such parties directly. One of the main economic justifications for the middle man in this and many other situations is the difficulty of finding a match directly. Professionals who take the risk on their books while they seek out a counterparty make the perfect match possible in the long run. Possible but not certain; one reason for some of the more complicated swaps is the failure to find a direct match; the bank may then have to do a series of swaps to end up with the right overall position.

One risk for all participants but particularly the professionals is that they may forget this essential point; the justification of any market, and the thing that makes it work, is the service to the customer. It is very easy for professionals to think that they are making money solely out of their ability to outfox other professionals – or worse still to outguess the market. But whatever may be true of one professional, it cannot be true of all. When dealing with each other, professionals are in a zero sum game; the gains must be matched exactly by losses. Since both winners and losers have administrative costs and overheads, a purely professional market must lose money overall. In practice of course no market is ever purely professional, but there are times when the professional share becomes excessive, or when professionals become disdainful of the customer and reluctant to deal with him. By doing so they make the market less attractive to the customer and push the external revenue towards another market. This in turn reduces the revenue available to their market and increases the number of market makers who must lose money.

The customer also suffers when this happens. In theory he has dealt with a professional who in turn has dealt, even if at several removes, with a natural counterparty. Both parties have paid a reasonable fee, or other form of payment, for the service provided;

there is always a credit risk, but at least their transaction has not added to it and may have reduced it marginally. If in practice he has dealt into a purely professional market, with little or no external input, the credit risk may be higher than he could reasonably expect.

The same type of point applies to currency swaps and forward exchange contracts. They provide protection against fluctuations in exchange rates in one direction but give up the chance of gain from the reverse movement. They also carry the credit risk of the bank or other counterparty.

Investors or traders who use options as a hedge also transform the previous trading risk into a credit risk, rather than removing risk altogether. If the party from whom, or exchange through which, they buy the option fails to meet it when called upon to do so, the hedge is invalid and the trading risk is back; in almost all cases the reason the counterparty cannot meet its obligations will be related to credit. Again, the chance that the transaction, or the bank's involvement in the particular market, will weaken the credit is less where the market acts as an intermediary between natural counterparties, rather than mainly professionally, with a large zero sum risk.

This adds particular point to the earlier comment about the risks where customers try to make money out of speculating in markets, rather than using the markets to buy a necessary service or protection. If the market is a mainly professional one, as described, the newcomer adds to the element of zero sum and therefore to the risk that someone will lose money. Since almost by definition he is new to the market, he is more likely than most to be the loser.

All products which change the risk carry this element of new risk. Furthermore all contracts for differences carry a reciprocal credit risk; they are thus different from loan contracts in that the customer has as much right and sometimes need to worry about the bank's credit standing as the other way around.

CHANGE IN FORM MAY REDUCE PROTECTION

A product which changes the form of risk, whether or not it transfers it in ways discussed in the previous section, may change the protections built into the original form. While this change usually applies to the bank, it may sometimes apply to the borrower/counterparty. For instance, many commentators look on FRNs as just another form of bank loan. The argument is partly that banks end up buying most

FRNs; partly perhaps that since bank loans themselves are increasingly transferable, it does not matter to the borrower what transfer mechanism is used; but mainly that the form of borrowing, for a fixed period but with rates reset periodically, is similar to the old, often syndicated, floating rate bank loan.

The FRN obviously has advantages to the borrower, the most important of which is price; but it also has disadvantages. These can be looked at as lack of protection in certain areas, arising from lack of flexibility. For example, most bank facilities carry the right to vary the interest period; at least they give the choice between three and six months, and often a wider range. Despite some of the gimmicks in FRNs (use of the six month rate, but reset every month for instance), this type of flexibility is impossible with an FRN.

Fixed rate bonds provide the issuer with protection from rising interest rates, but carry the same disadvantages as an FRN in other areas. Issuers of all types of bonds, fixed or FRN, lose the protection of borrowing from banks which have a broader relationship. In normal times this may not be crucial; the borrower can have a relationship apart from the bond which will give it what it needs. In times of difficulty, however, a borrower needs lenders who understand its business. Ideally they should have a vested interest in avoiding precipitate action which would damage the borrower. Most eurobonds and FRNs are bearer securities, so that the borrower does not even know who the holders are. The difficulty of presenting an argument or proposal to keep the borrower alive and improve the chances of recovery has already been covered.

Nobody yet really knows how serious these points are, since, as discussed earlier, investment banks have successfully kept most bond issues out of reschedulings. (Dome Petroleum of Canada is a partial exception to this point; at first it had difficulty in bringing its bondholders into the restructuring of its debt, but succeeded in the end. It is too soon to tell whether the difficulty or ultimate success is the more important pointer.) With the explosive growth of bond issues this is no longer acceptable, since the amounts involved are often larger than the banks can justify to protect their own relatively smaller exposure.

For the bank the change in risk relates to the documentation. With a loan there will be clearly spelled out events of default. These give the bank a handle, when things are going wrong, to push management in the direction the bank thinks most likely to protect its loan. In a syndicate no one bank can do this, and a bank which takes a gloomier view than others may be overruled; nevertheless the syndicate has the same interests and can move as a unit, particularly if there is a strong agent to give a lead. FRNs lack both covenants and any prospect of a coherent group of experienced lenders with compatible views of the problem.

The justification for giving up the protection is the change from an illiquid to a liquid asset. There are genuine benefits, particularly when the FRN is seen as a way of managing interest rate risk rather than a conventional loan with a liquid feature. Nevertheless liquidity is in a sense a zero sum game; no one can sell unless someone else buys. Given that the FRN does not mature for several years, someone is going to need the protection of covenants, events of default, agents or trustees to co-ordinate action and so on. Liquidity does not change that fact; at most it changes the identity of the someone.

The same point arises in a slightly different form with NIFs, RUFs and MOFs. The underwriting bank normally does not need to lend, and to that extent may seem to get its fees for nothing. The buyers of the paper (often also banks) get the benefit of short-term paper with the underwriting banks to provide the medium-term commitment that the borrower needs. Since the paper is medium-term but at short-term rates there is a trade-off between protections. The investor wants the events of default to be as loose as possible; if the borrower goes downhill fast, or more gradually but less noticeably, he wants the maximum time to notice this and get out. The underwriter on the other hand is taking the long-term risk for very little return; he wants to be as sure as possible that he can accelerate before it is too late; yet if he makes this too obvious the holders will notice and not buy. Or at least that ought logically to be the case. In practice few underwriting banks seem to feel they need to worry about covenants; and few holders even seem to be aware of whether there are covenants, let alone their implications. Perhaps this is not so much a case of protections changing without those at risk noticing as of people losing protections they did not even know they could have.

This chapter tries to highlight the main areas where credit risk can be overlooked or misunderstood. It does not pretend to be a catalogue of all such risks, but a guide to the major ones and a pointer to ways of looking at risk to see what is concealed.

Part II

Details of Risk

4 Credit and Related Risk

GLOSSARY

Clearance risk A subdivision of settlement risk where settlement is through a clearing house. Risk either arises from the clearing house rules, or from failure of the clearing house itself.

Contract risk The risk that the bank has taken a wrong view and tied itself into a contract which may cost more than the possible gains justify. (Distinguish between contract and documentation risk: in one the bank gets the contract it intended, and regrets it; in the other the contract is not what it expected.)

Daily settlement limit A limit to the value of transactions with a given counterparty which a bank allows to settle on each day. This is separate from any limit on the total amount which may be outstanding.

Delivery *v.* payment (DVP) The delivery of securities or other assets against simultaneous payment in cash. In practice this is only possible where both parties are in the same centre or through a computerized clearing house. Many systems which purport to be DVP in fact are not; either payment is made by cheque, which can bounce; or it is made separately, so that one side has to deliver the asset before being sure of receipt of the cash. Hence the use of the phrase 'guaranteed DVP' in this book to cover DVP only in its full sense.

Documentation risk The risk that poor drafting or other weakness will make a contract invalid or unenforceable; or that the document will bind the bank in some way it did not intend, or fail to bind the client as the bank did expect; or that unclear or complicated drafting will cause mistakes by those who have to operate it.

Master agreement Where all transactions of a particular type between two parties are covered by one agreement. The details specific to each transaction will be spelt out in a 'confirmation', but the fundamental terms and conditions are contained in the master. Since everything is under one contract, the amounts owing can often be netted against each other, perhaps even in liquidation.

Operating risk The risk from operating mistakes. These can cause, or increase, credit risk; or they can create direct loss or liability unconnected to credit.

THE RISK OF A LOAN OR DIRECT CREDIT (LENDING RISK)

Lending risk covers all facilities which can give rise to a loan as well as loans themselves: revolving and standby commitments; unused overdrafts or other short-term or uncommitted facilities; letters of credit, guarantees and similar instruments which can lead to a loan; acceptances and bills discounted; commercial paper or any similar instrument which achieves roughly the same thing; bonds, whether fixed or floating; and any other way of extending credit which is expected to end up as a loan or could do so in a crisis.

The prime risk in lending is of loss of the face amount of the loan. In practice, banks try to ensure that they will not lose the whole face value, but can only make it unlikely, not impossible. Exposure as earlier defined spells out the maximum amount which could be lost, and the amount to which any percentage loss will apply. With a £1 million loan any loss will be a percentage of that amount.

Bankers often think of the lost principal as the whole loss. Sometimes it is, but more often it is merely the largest item. The most common additional item at risk is interest. It is in one sense double counting to look at the loss of interest separately, since it is one factor which gives value to the loan; if the asset ceases to have value, loss of income from it is part of that loss. But banks can lose interest as a way of preserving value in the asset and eventually recovering part of it. It is common in restructurings, for instance, to forgive part or all of the interest to recover principal. Where interest is not forgiven outright, it may be paid in shares or long-term or subordinated paper. The lender thus keeps alive the possibility of getting his interest back one day, but in a way which preserves the borrower's cash.

In a successful restructuring the banks may, years later, sell or convert the paper at a price that compensates them for the delay. More often they recover only a small proportion; quite often the restructuring either fails altogether, or succeeds only in the limited sense that the banks get back a higher share of the principal than they would have without the effort, but recover none of the interest forgone. In brief, loss of interest can be instead of, or as well as, loss of principal. In less extreme cases interest may not be lost in any final sense, but may be delayed, giving it a lower present value.

Management time and expenses are high in problem loans, which take great time and effort, run up large bills for lawyers and other experts; an international problem may also need travel and hotel bills. Apart from management time, these items are usually quite small in relation to the loan, although legal fees can be a larger percentage of a small loan, and can run to hundreds of thousands of dollars on a large one. They are recoverable from the borrower, but this is rarely much help.

Three other types of loss are less frequent but more serious when they occur. They could be called the asset liability risk, the shadow director risk and the lender liability risk.

The asset liability risk most often relates to secured debt, and applies when the lender takes control of or responsibility for the assets pledged. He may then find that he is liable for costs related to the asset, as in the shipping example mentioned in Chapter 3. Similar examples arise for property; there is also a risk that an unsound building which was not properly insured could cause damage or injury for which the bank would be liable. A bank taking a charge over receivables might even find itself facing product liability claims in some countries. Fortunately these risks are well recognized and lawyers can protect banks against the worst of them most of the time. Nevertheless they remain a factor for banks to consider, if only to be sure of avoiding them. None apply exclusively to secured debt, but they are more frequent with it.

Leasing is particularly risky here, since by definition the lessor owns the asset. Third party liability on an aircraft is only one example of the risks leasing companies face. Another is the risk from recent legislation in the United States, under which mortgagors can be liable for the cost of decontaminating land from toxic wastes. Banks are reported to be giving up security rather than face this risk, and one is thought to have lost many millions when it recognized the risk too late.

The shadow director risk arises when banks become too heavily involved in a company. The details vary from country to country, but there is usually some risk of the bank being adjudged to have influenced the company too much, or in some way to have misled other creditors. This in turn can make the bank liable for the losses of other creditors, or occasionally even criminally liable. Most countries recognize that there is a difference between running a company and trying to recover debt, even by getting more involved than usual. Not all countries' laws are clear on just exactly where the dividing line falls; in some countries, including Britain, the law has been recently reformed. It may be even harder to avoid risk until the courts interpret the new rules.

The lender liability risk overlaps with the other two to some extent, since either can give rise to a liability by the lender. In this paragraph, however, we use lender liability to cover a liability arising from actual or alleged mistakes or worse by the bank. The borrower may use the mistake to try to deny the obligation; or he may claim misbehaviour by the bank which mitigates or cancels the liability. Borrowers often claim, for instance, that a bank officer told them that the bank would not enforce covenants; or a guarantor that the bank promised not to call the guarantee. Or the borrower may claim that the bank used threats to force action which the borrower would not otherwise have taken; or that the bank withdrew its facility without due notice or in bad faith and prevented the borrower meeting its obligations. There may be claims by third parties against the bank arising from this or the borrower may itself claim damages.

Lender's liability in this context falls into three types. If the borrower's claim is true, the bank is deservedly at risk. More probably, the bank did not act in the way claimed, but was not careful enough in its behaviour to eliminate any suspicion that it did. Finally, there may be no truth in the claim, but the bank may not have recorded what happened well enough to prove its good faith. In addition to any liability to the borrower or third parties, a bank which is agent to a syndicate may also face claims for negligence from the other members.

The best protection against such claims is always to act in meticulous good faith and to document fully the basis on which the bank acts. To be completely effective, banks may need to do this to an extent which may seem ridiculous, and sometimes even offensive. Even less extreme measures of clear speaking and record keeping should let the bank win in the end; however, because good faith is as hard to prove conclusively as bad faith is easy to allege, banks risk time-consuming litigation harmful to their reputation. To avoid this they may settle out of court claims which they should win. (Where banks act in outright bad faith, rather than inadvertently, they deserve to lose money. In one case in the United States, for instance, a group of banks extracted harsh terms from a troubled borrower by threatening to bankrupt it if it refused; at the same time the banks agreed among themselves that it would not be in their best interest to do so. Although this can happen in lending as well as other aspects of business, it is then strictly a bad faith rather than a lending risk.)

And finally there is the lending risk that has nothing to do with credit. The most obvious example is the decision to finance a hostile bid for a client of the bank. The target may sue the bank for misuse of confidential information. Even short of this, it will probably cut the relationship with the bank; where the bid fails this may lead to the loss of future profits. It can also upset other clients and lose profits that way.

SETTLEMENT RISK

Settlement risk is of two types: direct risk, covering the whole value of one side of the transaction; and market risk. Where a counterparty fails to deliver but the bank avoids the direct risk, it still has to replace the transaction. If the market moves against it, this can cause a loss, the maximum size of which depends on several variables. And of course the two can be combined. A bank which delivers bonds and is not paid has to replace the bonds. If the price rises the cost is more than the original purchase price.

Direct risk

Direct risk is greatest where the transaction is settled in different centres or even time zones. In practice the latter often means foreign exchange deals, or derivatives such as swaps and long-dated currency exchanges. Delivery against payment, which is the best protection where available, is rarely possible in these cases. With different time zones, the first payer may not even know whether the other side has paid until the next day, or for several days over a weekend or holiday. A bank which sells sterling and buys dollars normally takes a greater settlement risk than one dealing the other way, which can know whether it has received the sterling before it has to pay the dollars. (In theory at least; it is impracticable to check all the time, although banks can do so exceptionally where there is real doubt as to the counterparty's ability to pay.)

In other cases it may be possible in theory to deliver against payment but not in practice. This is most often true with securities where good delivery is physical delivery. Some clearing houses, such as Euroclear and Cedel, are fully computerized and can match payment against delivery. Even here, however, the parties are involved in some clearance risk (see below). Excluding these cases, direct settlement risk is greatest where there is a settlement or clearance system imposed by the local stock exchange or sometimes by law.

These systems were originally set up to handle a relatively small volume among counterparties who were all members of the local exchange or community. They knew each other well and gained more from the idiosyncrasies of the system than they lost. The deregulation of exchanges in many countries and the growing international interest in domestic exchanges has changed this. The greater volume has converted a minor risk into a significant one; and the participants are more numerous, less well known to each other and less inclined to play by unwritten rules which they do not understand.

International firms and banks, for instance, dislike the requirement of the International Stock Exchange (formerly the London Stock Exchange) that shares to be delivered out of Talisman on Monday must be delivered into it by the previous Friday. With an agency sale Talisman will deliver a cheque in favour of the selling client to the selling broker; while less than ideal, this should avoid the cheque being included in the broker's assets if it fails at the crucial time. Where the broker acts as principal, however, which he could not do before Big Bang, payment is independent of Talisman. Normally the broker is unable to pay outright until he in turn has been paid on Monday on delivery of the shares to the buyer. The practice has now grown up of giving the seller a post-dated cheque on Friday, which will clear on Monday – or not, as the case may be. The Exchange is even pressing international clients to deliver on Thursday and accept an extra day of exposure.

The situation in Paris is worse in mid-1988, however, although improvements are said to be due shortly. Here the shares are delivered to the clearing house (Sicovam) and the money to the Banque de France. The seller does not know until the following day whether the Banque has its money; a buyer does not know until the third day whether the Sicovam has the shares. There are many other variants and in some of them the bank cannot take security on the shares being delivered or other shares it holds.

Banks take settlement risk in one of three capacities. They can do it as a principal to the transaction, where they themselves have bought or sold. Investment banks in some countries have always done this, although in others this may be the result of recent changes which have reduced the difference between a market maker and an agency broker. Commercial banks in many cases have only begun to do it recently with securities as they expand into investment banking, although they have always done it in the foreign exchange markets. Most commercial banks have a system for setting forward exchange limits for counterparties, whether other banks or clients. They do not all have spot exchange lines, although these or daily settlement lines are becoming more frequent. There seems to be no standard way of setting and controlling settlement lines for the securities business.

Banks also incur settlement risk by running a settlement service for clients, mostly brokers. Here they take in securities or cash with instructions to deliver or receive against payment. Either way the bank accepts the responsibility to make the system work, and at least some of the risk to which the particular system gives rise.

Finally they can act as custodian, and deliver as agent. Here the risk is normally for the account of the client on whose behalf they hold the shares, particularly where the client has chosen which broker to use. Nevertheless banks need to be careful. If the instruction is to deliver against payment, they may not be able to do so, but may believe they are bound to follow the market's custom and can assume that the customer accepts it. Unless the market practice is well known, and probably even then, it is as well to spell out the rules to the client. Where the custom is changing, he must know of and accept the change in risk. Failing this, or if it makes an operating mistake, the bank may be held liable for the client's losses.

In all capacities, the bank must make sure that it knows how the particular settlement system works, what are the risks involved, and against which of them it can protect itself. Then it must decide that it can accept the risk remaining or pass it on to someone who will. It must also know what protections are available in an emergency, even those which would make the system unworkable if they became routine. For instance, taking the Talisman example given above, the bank can refuse to release the shares into Talisman until it has been paid. But, if the broker cannot get the shares without paying and cannot pay until he gets the shares, he is out of business. In practice, either he will borrow, transferring the risk to another bank which does not have the same control, or he will need to tie up more capital in the settlement system, making the whole process more expensive.

In brief, direct settlement risk is an essential lubricant to the markets. It may be largely eliminated eventually by computer matching systems, but until then banks serving, or active in, the securities industry have little choice but to accept it. To justify this, they must understand it, control it and risk the minimum necessary to keep the system working smoothly.

Market risk

Market risk in settlement arises when the counterparty fails but the bank avoids the direct risk; it loses, or occasionally gains, only the market movement between the bargain and the time when it replaces it. This period can vary from a few hours to weeks or even months. When the delay is more than a few weeks this usually suggests a breakdown in the settlement system.

In dealing in gilt-edged stocks in London, for instance, market makers settle with each other the following business day, through the Central Gilts Organisation. The market risk here is for 24 hours only. The maximum loss, if the bank reacts promptly, is the price movement of the gilt during that 24-hour period, almost certainly below five per cent; anything close to that would imply a catastrophic market. The London Stock Exchange runs account periods of two or three weeks for equities during which, as October 1987 showed, a volatile share could move more than 25 per cent; in more normal times, perhaps 15–20 per cent.

In New York the settlement period is five days; in various European centres it can be as much as six weeks. When settlement systems are weak the official period may have little contact with reality. In Italy at one time the average settlement took between six months and a year. Morgan Guaranty established Euroclear in the 1960s because settlement in the eurobond market was averaging over six months with periods up to eighteen months quite common and two years possible. The risk was so great that the market might not have survived without Euroclear.

Market settlement risk thus depends on the rules of the settlement system; on whether it works; on the volatility of the market concerned; on how easy it is to buy in or sell out; on how easy it is to be sure that there has been a failure to settle, rather than an acceptable delay. The actual loss, if any, in cases where the counterparty fails will depend on which way the market moves. Where a bank buys an equity share at 100 and the counterparty fails to deliver, the bank will lose nothing if the price of the share moves to 95 before it buys in; if the price moves to 110, the cost will be considerable. The reverse is true when the bank sells.

There is a version of lender's liability involved in buying in. Most formal exchanges have rules about when this is permissible and how to do it; on over-the-counter exchanges this may not always be true. Even where there are such rules, they may not always be wholly clear, and may not have been tested in the courts. To buy in too soon may leave the bank open to a claim for damages if the counterparty subsequently wants to deliver, claims it was always able to do so, and that the bank had no right to buy in. To refrain from buying in for fear of this risks the market moving further against the bank, thus increasing the loss if the counterparty is a genuine defaulter.

CLEARANCE RISK

There are three types of clearance risk. One is the risk caused by the clearing house rules. In one sense this is merely another way of looking at direct settlement risk; the Talisman and Paris examples mentioned in the previous section are cases in point. However they are worth distinguishing because the clearing house rules either create the particular form of risk or at least prevent the bank from changing to a more secure method.

The clearing house may not have to cover any loss the bank incurs when the clearing house breaks its own rules whether deliberately, through negligence or even fraud. The greatest danger may not be fraud or accident, but well-meant design. The latest and most notorious case in point was the Tin Council collapse. The London Metal Exchange changed the rules so that contracts were settled at a price which would not bankrupt half the members of the exchange; unfortunately this was a price at which other members lost, at least, the profit they had expected.

Even in less drastic situations, banks need to be sure that the clearing house is liable for failure to follow its own rules. The rules may say that the clearing house will only release securities against cash. If the rules are followed, a bank which deposits cash to pay for securities will receive the securities or its cash back; and vice versa. If the clearing house in error releases securities when the buyer does not have the cash, is the clearing house liable? If not, the ultimate protection given is worth less than it seems. It is worth something, because an efficient clearing house will not make that mistake very often. But the apparent guarantee of payment or return of securities is no longer a guarantee, merely a high probability. This still may be easier and less risky than other forms of settlement, but it is not guaranteed DVP.

Lastly, the clearing house itself may collapse, involving banks and other parties in loss in two ways. The failure of the settlement system may leave the clearing house unable to meet the resulting liabilities, whether from failed settlements or because the clearing house itself gives credit as if it were a bank. If members can overdraw, a borrower's failure may drag the clearing house down; equally, if the clearing house pays out in error and is liable, this may break it. Then any client who has either securities or cash with the house may find itself unsecured. Even where the system works in a way that allocates assets to the owners rather than treating them as fungible, there is likely to be some delay while a liquidator sorts out who owns what. Or, as with the collapse of the Paris clearing house for sugar in the 1970s, there may be prolonged litigation before everybody knows exactly where they stand.

Clearing houses may cause loss for their members. Some are partnerships or have rules which make members liable as if they were partnerships. Others have a 'compensation fund' or similar arrangement to which members must contribute at need. Others do not have such an arrangement directly but are part of an exchange which is liable for their debts and which itself has some such arrangement. The need for brokers to replenish the guarantee fund of the Paris Bourse, following speculative losses announced in June 1988, was a good example of the risk this can involve. And some exchanges require members to deal with all other members, up to a minimum amount, and settle through the exchange's clearing house.

So in using clearing houses banks need to consider four main points:

(1) What are the rules of the house and how well or badly do they protect participants?
(2) What degree of legal obligation does the clearing house accept for failure to follow its rules?
(3) What is the credit standing of the clearing house?
(4) What are the obligations of membership?

In reviewing the credit standing banks need in turn to look at three main points:

(1) What is the direct financial strength of the clearing house? What assets does it have on hand, with what degree of liquidity, before it has to rely on shareholders or members?
(2) How does it hold the participants' assets? Are they all treated as fungible (which is probably the most efficient operationally)? Or

are the securities segregated so that in liquidation the owner of each asset can identify it? (Cash is so inherently fungible that it is doubtful whether any system could segregate it.) Even where securities are fungible, the law may allow partial allocation. For instance, ten participants may deposit between them one million units of a particular security, which nobody else holds. It is then clear that none of these securities belong to anyone else. Depending on the law of the particular country, the ten may then be able to divide the holding between them *pro rata* to what they deposited; if there is a shortfall, they will share it *pro rata* and be unsecured creditors for the remaining amount only.

(3) What are the obligations of members and how great is their ability to meet them? This is important to users of the system who want to assess their risk, and to members. The latter need to know their obligation, the extent to which they can be additionally liable if other members fail to meet their share, and the risk of this failure.

With both settlement and clearing house risk, and to a lesser extent with some of the other risks discussed in this book, there is an argument that the outline above may overstress the risk. Each individual risk is short-term, there have been few failures, and there are political and other reasons for believing that the financial community or government would bail out any clearing house. (For banks which qualify as the 'financial community', that part of the argument may not be so comforting.) The settlement risk in foreign exchange is often referred to as the Herrstatt risk precisely because that is the only public case where banks have lost money in this way.

Furthermore, the argument might run, banks must take these risks to make the financial system work. Unless someone pays out at the beginning, the chain of transactions can never complete itself; unless it is expected to complete it will never start and activity will grind to a halt, leaving the banks with more risk than anything they have avoided by refusing settlement risk.

There is some truth in this, but it is too black and white. First, it is true that any individual settlement risk is short-term; a bank would be very unlucky if it settled one transaction for a client on the day the client failed. But banks rarely settle just once for a client which they then never see again. They settle daily, weekly or monthly over a long time. If the client fails they are almost sure to be settling something when he does so.

Secondly, the sheer volumes are too great; such an attitude, even if it ever was justified, now no longer is. After all, if the banking system is bankrupted by the risk, all the consequences of refusing to handle the transactions will be superimposed on the effects of a shattering financial crash, comparable to 1929 and 1987. These risks are most clearly seen in the New York market, where leading banks face daylight overdrafts for other banks and for securities houses running into billions of dollars per client; in a few cases the risk on each of several clients may be more than the bank's net worth. However small the chance of loss, that risk is one no bank should take without maximum precautions. The risks in settling securities (other than commercial paper which gives rise to some of the volume in the New York clearing) may not run into quite such large figures individually, but they are still large and the cumulative figures run into many billions of dollars. Largest of all are the amounts going through CHIPS (Clearing House International Payment System), where the leading New York banks clear the foreign exchange and other transactions for overseas banks.

The third and most important reason for examining these risks closely is to guard against three types of mistake a bank can make about risk. It can underestimate risk, and lose money it should not lose; it can overestimate risk and lose profitable business it should take; or it can take a greater risk than necessary because it either neglects simple precautions or mistakes the risk it takes for another.

For instance, it is probably true that, given a half-way efficient settlement system, the risk in handling settlements of the sale or purchase of securities is not very great; the risk in lending to facilitate that settlement is not much greater. There are, however, several provisos to that statement, and the risk is only as low as appears at first glance if the provisos are met. The first is the comment about a half-way efficient settlement system. Some systems are or have been so inefficient that users run greater risk than is reasonable.

Secondly, all secured settlement risk is self liquidating, with two possible ways out. The expected way is the completion of the transaction; even if the market moves against the bank, this will not matter if the original counterparty completes at the original price. If the counterparty fails the bank still has the charge over the assets which it can sell to repay the loan, but to take full advantage of this in a fast-moving market takes skill and attention. In a catastrophic market, such as occurred in October 1987, even the most alert bank may sell at a loss. Less alert banks can suffer larger losses in smaller falls.

Thirdly, settlement risk is lower because most banks only lend secured and with a safety margin, to ensure that they will be paid even if settlement fails. The price of the security may move before they discover that the counterparty will not settle; the margin should be set to cover the greatest likely move until the bank can buy in or sell out. A bank which takes settlement risk too lightly may think it unnecessary to secure itself. Apart from the lower protection this may also mean that it considers what the risk is, and how best to protect itself, including when to take security and how to realize it, less thoroughly than it should. Full consideration of risk and protection makes disaster less likely in three ways.

First, it ensures that, when disaster threatens, the bank is fully aware both of the risk and of how best to minimize it. If it needs to move fast, it is prepared to do so; this makes it less likely that it will lose anything, and most unlikely that it will lose heavily. A bank that is not alert may not recognize the need for swift action; may not know whether it has the legal right to take action, or may not have that right.

Secondly, a bank that knows the risks and how to protect itself is less likely to panic and take precipitate action which may undermine the market just when it most needs support. In the October 1987 crash some banks which had lent unsecured to the brokerage industry either withdrew their lines or seriously considered doing so. In one sense, of course, they were quite right; the last time to get caught with unsecured borrowings to brokers is in the middle of a panic. But in a more important sense they were entirely wrong; the surest way to turn a panic into a major disaster is to remove liquidity from the market. This cuts the ground from under the feet of firms which, however sound, depend on continuing liquidity for survival. Banks which do not want to get caught lending unsecured to a broker in the middle of a crash should think of that well before the crash starts.

Finally, lending unsecured and without proper understanding of the risks may actually encourage brokers to take unsound risk themselves. If so this increases the danger of a failure with wider repercussions. The theory of lending to brokers is that the loans support liquid assets in transactions that are either fully self liquidating or close to it. Loans may cover the period of settlement, or perhaps different settlement periods in separate markets; or banks may finance the holding, for a few days or weeks only, of assets which they expect will be sold and the proceeds used to pay the loan. The risk of market fluctuation should be financed with equity not debt.

The banks ensure this by taking the margin already described and thus forcing the broker to have a level of equity appropriate to the level of business he is doing. Moreover, by insisting on higher margin for less liquid securities or more risky transactions, banks can ensure that the capital fits the quality of business as well as the volume.

In theory, if all banks are unsecured, and the broker keeps the same margin of capital, the banks should be in almost the same position in liquidation as if they were all secured on sound assets, with a margin which required the same level of capital. In practice, however, most brokers will relax their capital standards once they can borrow unsecured. Banks which agree to lend unsecured thus fail to enforce sound standards, adding to their own risk, and to that of the market and the borrower. And agreement to lend unsecured often relates back to the feeling that settlement risk is not, after all, so very serious.

DOCUMENTATION RISK

There are several types of documentation risk: legal, commercial and operational/complexity. Although it is sensible to discuss them separately, they often interact with each other. Legal risk causes loss when the bank cannot enforce the agreement in the law courts, or is uncertain enough about its case to settle rather than sue. Usually this failure will relate to a particular aspect rather than the whole document. For instance, a guarantee or charge on collateral may be invalid, while the debt remains. Or the court may refuse to accelerate the debt while accepting that there is a valid obligation to pay. In a few cases the failure may be more important; if the court rules invalid a guarantee which is the main source of repayment, the loss may be almost as great as if it invalidated the loan. Equally, it may rule one bank's security invalid and another's valid. The loser may then find that documentation risk leaves it unsecured behind a secured lender, which can cause heavy loss.

Less serious risks may cover penalty interest; a bank may recover the full loan and normal interest but not penalty interest for a late payment. Or the documentation may not protect against the costs of new reserve or capital adequacy regulations.

Legal risk can have one of four main causes, or a mixture of any two or more of them. The first is straightforward negligence or incompetence by the lawyer drafting the agreement. Unless the banker has legal training, or the error is obvious, few bankers can be expected to catch this; the only solution is to employ good lawyers. In theory this type of mistake leaves the lawyer open to damages; most lawyers carry insurance against such claims and will settle a strong case. But if they do not settle it can be hard to prove negligence.

The second is poor communication between the lawyer and the banker. The lawyer does not fully understand what the banker wants, and the banker fails to notice that he has not got it. This may be bad luck or misunderstanding. More often, it arises from poor banking; while not a lawyer, the banker should understand the agreement well enough to assess its impact and recognize where it does not do what he wanted. In particular, the banker must give the lawyer clear instructions; without these the lawyer cannot get the first draft right, and it is much harder to change tack than to get on the right one in the first place.

This type of mistake may relate to withholding tax, for instance; many borrowers who agree to pay interest gross (that is, absorb the cost of withholding tax) insist on a clause entitling them to a refund if the bank subsequently recovers any of it. Many banks are happy to concede this. Some, mostly American, have major problems because of the way their tax laws work, the complexity of their tax position, and the delays in settling the tax bill. Some banks will not (or at one stage would not) accept the clawback clause at all; others will accept it in limited circumstances, and in wording that fits their requirements exactly. A lawyer who has not worked for the bank before and a banker who does not recognize the importance of the point can commit the bank to a position which breaches its policy.

The third cause is a change in regulations, law or market practice which could not have been, or at least was not, foreseen when the agreement was drafted. One reason why agreements are so long is that there have been many such changes over the years; each time the lawyers come across one, they draft a new clause to cover it. This type of mistake is particularly dangerous in syndication, whether in lending or capital markets; the agent or manager can lay himself open to risks through negligence, or new interpretations of what constitutes negligence, unless the agreement specifically protects him.

This may be important with loan sales, a new area which can shade over into the security laws which are themselves being revised in many countries. Either the laws change, or the interpretation; either way, transactions which were documented as loan sales may be caught under rules primarily aimed at something different. Or, since one advantage of loan sales is to get the loan off balance sheet, new regulations may require the sale agreement to meet criteria nobody had thought of when it was drafted. The Bank of England published a consultative paper on the treatment of loan sales for capital adequacy in December 1987, which may have this effect. The Bank is a part of the Basle group of central banks which are working to agree common capital adequacy standards; other central banks may set similar standards – unless a hostile reaction causes the Bank to change its proposals.

The fourth area of legal risk is cross-border risk. Where more than one country is involved some aspects of the transaction may not be decided by the law of the agreement. For instance, if a Spanish company borrows in the euromarkets under English law, Spanish bankruptcy law still rules if the borrower fails; Spanish company law and exchange control will decide whether the borrower can do various things to which it commits in the agreement; and unless the borrower has assets outside Spain, Spanish courts will decide whether to enforce English law. Even with an English court judgment in hand, it matters whether the Spanish courts simply accept the judgment, or whether they will review it. If the latter, the bank must accept that Spanish courts do not recognize any cause for acceleration other than non-payment when due.

Indeed bankers from both systems must recognize that civil and common laws take different approaches to contract law and in particular to covenants in loan agreements. In essence, the common law view is that, if two parties freely contract to do something, they should be taken to have known what they were doing, and held to it; the civil law view is that the judge must decide in each case whether the contract is reasonable and will only enforce it if he feels he should. The reaction of judges to ratio and other covenants varies from country to country and even from judge to judge; no banker should assume that, just because his agreement says he can accelerate if a ratio is breached, he can actually do so. (Do not make the mistake, however, of thinking that, because you cannot enforce a covenant, it is not worth having; the ability to enforce has never been the only or even the major argument in favour of covenants.)

Sometimes borrowers have assets in several different countries. An unsecured agreement will not change much from a purely domestic borrower; the points about the ability to enforce will still apply, particularly if the assets are held through subsidiaries rather than directly. If banks need guarantees or charges over foreign assets, however, the documentation becomes highly complex, with a rising risk of mistakes.

Some legal opinions, which say that an agreement is enforceable in a particular country, may mean merely that a judge can enforce the agreement; they may omit to point out that he need not do so if he finds it unreasonable. This may be inherent in the legal system and thus not seem to need saying; a common law reader who expects the law to enforce valid contracts, and to assess their validity rather than their fairness, may not appreciate the point.

The commercial risk in documentation is arguably not a true documentation risk at all, in the sense of risk due to poor drafting. However there are some points which arise only when discussing the draft, rather than as part of the commercial negotiations which precede it. In the broader negotiations they may be covered only by a phrase such as 'subject to documentation normal for this type of facility' or 'subject to standard euromarket documentation'. Even where the heads of agreement mention a clause, it will be in outline: 'interest to be paid gross' or 'standard changes in circumstances wording, including capital adequacy'. The clause can still take different forms. Where it aims to protect against possible future changes in law or regulation, it can easily get mixed up with the point made earlier about failing to cover unforeseen eventualities.

One reason that these areas are left to the detailed drafting is that they often protect against remote possibilities rather than existing risks or costs; these will be covered fully in the commercial negotiations. Thus the withholding tax point mentioned earlier is often negotiated bitterly where no withholding tax is in force. With an existing tax the parties know the exact circumstances, and can agree a commercial deal to cover them. With no withholding now in place, or expected, both parties seek to protect themselves against a notional worsening in their position. Or, which can be worse, a lawyer tries too hard to protect his client without knowing whether the point is important to him. Sometimes indeed lawyers, consciously or otherwise, try to renegotiate something the client has already agreed; this is more dangerous than such lawyers seem to recognize. It throws doubt on their client's good faith and may make the bank reluctant to concede on more important points.

Similar comments apply to, say, the changes in circumstances clause. Neither side really expects the Federal Reserve or the Bank of England to impose additional reserve requirements, or make certain types of loan illegal, retroactively; or the euromarkets to dry up so that banks cannot get quotes on six-month dollars. But when negotiating a five- or seven-year loan, neither side can be sure that it will not happen, and therefore the agreement must cover it.

The nature of the commercial risk involved in this type of documentary point thus often seems slight. The bank, and the borrower, must balance a risk which may seem largely academic against the risk of irritating a good client and perhaps weakening its negotiating position elsewhere. And yet the bank has to recognize the importance of precedent and equal treatment of clients. If it gives way on the point to one client, it probably must do so to clients of comparable standing, and even of lesser standing. In other words, for most companies the loss if they concede and events work against them is quite small; for banks on the other hand the loss, though unlikely, can be very large. Banks usually cannot, or at least should not, take the risk. If all banks recognized this and dug in their heels the world would be an easier place for bankers. However, they do not; there are always some companies which resist even standard market practices, and some banks which concede.

The number of contentious points grows when the documentation covers contracts for differences, such as swaps. Here the obligations are reciprocal, and some strong corporate credits will refuse to give certain clauses unilaterally. A bank then has to decide whether it will, for instance, give a cross default clause in order to get one from the counterparty; or whether to do without either. Both can carry risks; banks are engaged in such a wide range of transactions that it is almost inevitable that they will sometimes be in technical default. The default may be due to an administrative error or to a dispute. If it can be used to bring down every other agreement to which the bank is a party the risk becomes simply unacceptable. On the other hand, to enter into a major long-term credit arrangement with any but the best corporate without protection may be to take too high a risk.

There is no simple answer to this or the various other clauses which give rise to dispute. The relative credit rating of the banks and counterparties is crucial. Until the 1980s, banks were strong enough to override objections from most borrowers; companies mostly accepted that the banks' credit standing was so high that there was no serious risk in the then fewer reciprocal arrangements, even if they rejected some of the other arguments. It is no longer axiomatic, however, that all banks are undoubted credits. Some banks are clearly weaker than many corporates, and even the strongest banks tend to be seen as slightly weaker than the strongest corporates. Add this to the natural tendency of corporates to want a better deal from their bank than their competitors can get, and the competitive pressure on banks to get business, and we have a recipe for banks to give more than they should.

There are several approaches banks can take, other than genuflection. They can be combined in various ways. One is to limit the cross default to swaps – or even to swaps with the same bank, where there is no master agreement. The master agreement is another partial answer. It brings all swaps between the bank and a particular counterparty under one agreement, and makes a default on any swap a default on the master agreement. This in effect gives a cross default between all swaps covered by the master, but without being objectionably explicit. (A master agreement has more important advantages from both points of view. It allows for netting of payments and, banks hope, of obligations in bankruptcy; this reduces the amount at risk in both directions. It also allows one agreement to be negotiated, rather than a whole series; once a master is in place, each new swap is documented by a simple confirmation, which gives the details – amount, currencies, interest rates, maturity and other payment dates, and so on – but otherwise simply adopts the terms of the master.)

Banks can limit the cross default so that it applies only where the sum covered is above a certain level. This may be an absolute amount, or a percentage of the parties' equity. The latter has the advantage that it reflects the difference in size of the counterparties, and will change as that size changes. Thus if a major bank prefers a fixed sum, it will find it hard to choose one which is small enough for a \$100mn client without being absurdly restrictive on the bank; if the bank uses, say, 3 per cent of equity this may be over one hundred million dollars for the bank and only a million or two for the small corporate. Nevertheless the relative importance of the default will be similar in both cases.

It is ironic that banks should be forced into this position. Before the days of swaps, they usually rejected any size limitation on cross default, on the grounds that a small amount was easily manageable and therefore failure to meet it had implications about the overall situation more serious than failure to manage a larger amount. These arguments remain valid, but banks are now seeing the other side more clearly: the danger of a default arising from administrative error, or in some small branch or subsidiary without management being aware until too late.

However, the purpose of this section is not to list all the contentious clauses in every possible type of agreement, but to highlight the ways in which commercial risk can arise in documentation. There is some overlap with the legal risk already discussed; in a number of cases the error could arise either through poor legal drafting or because the banker gave way in the commercial negotiations. One factor which increases commercial risk in documentation of swaps and other reciprocal transactions is that in some cases the basic deal has been done before the documentation is agreed. Commercially speaking, and perhaps legally, depending on the exact circumstances and country, the bank cannot change the deal without the counterparty's consent. Insistence on wording which the counterparty dislikes may therefore look like an attempt to change the deal through the back door. There is a growing market practice to use a standard set of swap terms and specify any exception at the time of dealing. (Indeed, in the London market the Bank of England insists on this practice.) The risk is then no longer of a banker being out-negotiated. Unless the dealer specifies the right terms at the time he deals, the banker may never be able to negotiate at all. And although the terms, just because they are standard, should be adequate in most respects, they will not cater for the weaker credits.

This whole area of reciprocal risk is in some ways less important when dealing with corporate counterparties than with financial ones. Not all of the latter are banks, and they are more likely to be dealers or even speculators in swaps and similar instruments than corporates are. Fortunately these are also the cases where it is easiest and most appropriate to have a master agreement; once this is in place, the dealers only have to say 'under the master between us' for any terms other than those relating to the exact transaction. To deal frequently with a counterparty where there is no master in place leaves too often two choices. Either there will be several elderly deals with no agreement in place, or a series of disputes about what documentation has been tacitly agreed or is needed; the disputes almost guarantee that agreements will be signed late, if ever.

Finally, under documentation risk we face operational/complexity risk. The operational risk is simply that the people who have to operate the document – calculate and make or receive the payments, give notices, control collateral, check compliance and so on – may fail in some way that causes the bank loss, or at least increases the chance of loss. It may take a combination of operating and some other risk to produce an actual loss in some cases; in others operations alone can do it.

Operational risk in this sense is often hard to distinguish from operating risk as described in the next section. The difference lies in the fact that the documentation in some way contributes to the operating error which leads to loss. Operating error can of course occur without the documentation being at fault. A clerk can misread even a straightforward clause, or garble sound instructions. Operational risk may be worse than necessary owing to complexity, to clumsy structure of the document or to poor definitions.

The transaction itself may be complex, or may be due to unnecessary frills put there for 'marketing reasons'. Equally, complex wording may be necessary to cover all the issue, but can be needlessly opaque. A major cause of operational risk in this sense is the attitude of lawyers to legal drafting. American lawyers are the worst offenders, at least in the author's experience, but English are not much better and almost all are bad. The problem stems from two sources.

The first is in itself desirable, but is carried too far. It is the idea that no agreement should come to court because the lawyers have failed to define what it is supposed to mean; and that, if it does come to court for other reasons, the argument will be about the facts of what happened, not about what the agreement meant to say. This is desirable in itself; indeed it is one of the key arguments used by the author, among others, for having a proper agreement. Unfortunately lawyers think of this as the sole reason, or at least the overriding one, and of other lawyers as the sole readers of the agreement. (This sweeping statement is a little unfair to a minority of lawyers, but is generally true; even those of whom it is less true tend this way but avoid the worst excesses.) However lawyers are not the sole readers; indeed, in most cases no lawyer looks at an agreement after it is signed. The bank clerks who use it are more or less experienced and educated, depending on the bank and the type of agreement, but rarely with any legal training.

The second point is that legal drafting (including parliamentary and congressional bills) has simply gone mad. In trying to cover every eventuality, and avoid the occasional ambiguous piece of punctuation, lawyers seem to have decided first that the only way to avoid missing out a point which relates to another is to put everything in one sentence; they refuse to cover related points in separate sentences in the same paragraph, or even in numbered subclauses. And secondly, that the best way to avoid ambiguous punctuation is to have no punctuation at all; some of them continue their sentences for so long that one begins to feel they are trying to abolish even the full stop.

The result is that some agreements consist mainly of, and most contain, sentences longer than the average paragraph in this book; often each such long sentence contains numerous sub-phrases with no punctuation to show to what they refer; equally often it incorporates half a dozen or more different concepts, which could each more easily be dealt with in a separate sentence. When the lawyers claim that all this is not just the best but the only way to make the meaning legally clear, non-lawyers may be forgiven a little scepticism. More importantly, they may wonder whether legal drafting which breaks all the norms of English grammar, style and sentence construction is not counterproductive in a commercial world. After all, if it is unclear to those who have to operate it, it may increase rather than reduce the chances of ending in court. (This may sound exaggerated; in the sense only that not all agreements are like this, and even the worst have some shorter, clearer sentences in them, perhaps it is. To prove that it is not wholly exaggerated, however, see the following quotation. This is taken from the ISDA standard master agreement for interest rate and currency swaps; it is part of an appendix which purports to define the method of calculating payments due if one party defaults during the life of a swap. This is one of the worst examples, but by no means the only one, of this type of wording in a document which is supposed to standardize and clarify:

> 'Market Quotation' means, with respect to a Swap Transaction and a party to the Swap Transaction making the determination, an amount (which may be negative) determined on the basis of quotations from Reference Market-makers for the amount that would be payable on the Early Termination Date, either by the party to the Swap Transaction making the determination (to be expressed as a positive amount) or to such party (to be expressed as a negative amount), in consideration of an agreement between such party and the quoting Reference Market-maker and subject to such documentation as they may in good faith agree, with a term commencing on the Early Termination Date (or, if later, the date specified in the relevant Confirmation as the date of commencement of such Swap Transaction) that would have the effect of preserving for such party the economic equivalent of the payment obligations of the parties in respect of such Swap Transaction that would, but for the occurrence of the Early Termination Date, fall due after such Early Termination Date (excluding any Unpaid Amounts in respect of such Swap Transaction but otherwise

including, without limitation, any amount that would, but for the occurrence of the Early Termination Date, have been payable (assuming each applicable condition precedent had been satisfied) on the next applicable payment date in respect of any period during which such Early Termination Date occurs.)

Of course the two types of complexity can reinforce each other; complicated or obscure drafting can make a complex transaction even harder to understand. Poor drafting of a complex agreement thus redoubles the chance of an operational error, and consequent loss. Poor drafting can be in the structure, as well as the wording, of the document, so that clauses which should interact with each other do not seem to do so; or items which logically belong in one part of the agreement are included in another and therefore more easily overlooked. For instance, most agreements have a section which covers the calculation of interest, fees and other charges. Sometimes, however, a clause covering a fee, or perhaps a contingent charge, will appear in another part of the agreement, where it is easy to overlook. Even the failure to give a simple index to the clauses can make it unnecessarily hard to find a point and add to the risk that it will be missed.

OPERATING RISK

Operating risk is the risk of loss from an operating error, for whatever reason. It thus includes the documentation/operational risk referred to in the previous section. Indeed, it is often difficult to distinguish between the two. It is rarely clear that an operating mistake arises solely from the complexity of the document, after all. There is usually an element of carelessness, inexperience or some other fault in the clerk who makes the mistake. All one can say for sure is that the complexity makes it less likely that the fault is all in the clerk; particularly where the problem is inexperience rather than basic incompetence, a clearly drafted document is less likely to cause such mistakes.

Simple mistakes can have simple consequences, such as a failure to claim a commitment fee when due. Or they can be less obvious, and have consequences which perhaps only become clear years later. Failure to check and enforce compliance on the covenants of a loan agreement may not seem to matter at first. If the covenant is too tight and is breached without the company getting into trouble, it may indeed not matter; the company will continue to pay interest and in due course principal until it has paid everything it owes. Some covenants, however, are well designed, so that a breach warns of a deterioration which sometimes continues to a critical stage. The operational failure to notice and act on the breach early may cost the bank its chance to recover its money before other creditors notice the deterioration; or to pressure management to take corrective action while it still might work. Or, when the bank finally wakes up to the breach of covenant and tries to use it to accelerate the loan, it may find it no longer can; its earlier failure to enforce may have acted as a constructive waiver, and the clause no longer have any force. (In the worst case the bank could then be sued for damages because its action precipitated the borrower's insolvency; a more likely case is that fear of this will inhibit the bank from pressing its case as hard as it otherwise would.)

In both these examples the error is connected in some way with credit, and the worst loss arises only when a credit risk also comes home to roost; the cost of a late commitment fee is not too severe if it is eventually paid, and failure to use a breached covenant to protect a loan is only expensive if there is a real weakness.

There are some errors where the cost is more than that of a pure credit risk, while still connected to credit; and others where the cost has nothing to do with any credit risk the bank takes directly. First, for example, when the bank is agent in a loan agreement; here an operational error may make it liable to reimburse the losses of all the syndicate members, at greater cost than where the bank was a sole lender. Secondly, the bank may be liable for customer losses caused by its own errors. Take the shipping industry in a period when charter rates rise sharply. Ships on charters fixed before the rise miss the opportunity to earn higher rates; their owners may be on the look-out for excuses to break the old charter and recharter at current rates. One such excuse is non-payment or late payment of the charter hire. Several major oil companies in one such period warned that they would hold the banks liable for any loss caused by late payment due to a bank mistake. Any loss by a client for this reason may give the client a claim against the bank; or the bank may pay to avoid damaging a good relationship, or incurring publicity which could harm its reputation. Sometimes this costs more than paying the client's losses.

In brief, whenever a bank undertakes operational services for a client it runs a risk of making costly mistakes. It is normally paid for such a risk, although banks used to perform more services free than is common today. But the payment does not always reflect the risk, and certainly does not reflect the added risk where a bank's operational management slips temporarily. And the nature and volume of operational services changes so fast that all banks seem to go through periods when parts of their operational services are below their normal standard.

SECURED, SENIOR OR SUBORDINATED

The different levels of seniority or security carry several types of risk: the risk of being less senior or secured than expected; the risk of being hurt by someone else's seniority or security; and the risk attached to the security or seniority. The value, or even validity, of security can be weakened or eliminated in three ways – poor documentation, lack of power to pledge and loss of value.

Poor documentation in this context means more than just the wording of the documents; it includes whatever is necessary to make and keep the pledge in full force and effect. Thus the document may fail to comply with legal requirements in some way, or leave out key points necessary to make it foolproof. Or the document may be in perfect form, but may need registration. In Britain, for instance, most types of security given by companies must be registered at Companies' House within twenty-one days of the charge becoming effective. Any charge which should be registered but is not is unenforceable against other creditors. There are also requirements for registering mortgages; other countries have similar requirements.

Alternatively the documentation may be valid but require monitoring in some way. Trust receipts, in some countries at least, fit this pattern. Given to the bank in return for documents of title – bills of lading or warehouse warrants in most cases – they contain undertakings to do something specific with the documents and return them, replace them or pay over the cash raised from them. For instance, clients use bills of lading, released under trust receipt, to remove goods from a ship, place them in a warehouse and deliver the warrants to the bank, which then continues to hold title to the underlying goods. However the process should only take a few days, and the bank should monitor to ensure that the warrants are delivered to it promptly, not kept and perhaps pledged to support other debt. Otherwise the trust receipt becomes stale and unenforceable, even without fraud. (In some countries, trust receipts either do not exist, or are not recognized by the courts as giving any valid claim, so that they are useless as security in any circumstances.)

Again the warrant that the bank holds may not be a document of title. In England, Holland and Germany, the chief issuers of warehouse warrants in Europe, there are different types of warrant. Some are fully negotiable documents of title; some are transferable but not negotiable; some are not even transferable, so that the warehouse may deliver the goods to the original depositor without seeing the warrant. Some also require some form of notice to become either negotiable or transferable. And the rules in each country are different.

These are only a few examples of the ways in which the banks can find that what they thought was a secured position is unsecured, or at best only partly secured. Secured lending requires constant vigilance and understanding of the rules governing the security: by the bankers who take the credit decision to approve the loan in the first place, and by those who operate the facility and check and value the security. This is always important but particularly in international finance; someone who knows the domestic law and practice well may too easily, but wrongly, assume that it applies in other countries.

Even where the documentation is sound the bank can still be unsecured if the borrower has no title to the goods pledged or no power to pledge them. Apart from fraud, which is a constant risk in lending but is not the subject of this book, this can happen in several ways. Take, for instance, reservation of title. This is a common concept in some continental European countries, given legal recognition in the United Kingdom by the Romalpa Case. Sale contracts may say that the goods remain the property of the seller until paid for in full or, in some cases, as long as the buyer owes the seller any money for whatever reason. In an extreme case the claim may extend not only to the underlying goods but to anything in which they are incorporated; bricks used to build a house could give their seller title to the whole house. In practice the courts are unlikely to go that far; in particular the position if the bricks were bought from two different sellers both of whom had a similar claim is unclear. Nevertheless the floating charge in Britain and similar forms of charge over a class of assets in other jurisdictions are threatened by reservation of title, since in many cases borrowers do not keep records of what comes with reservation and what without.

There are other ways, such as invalid title to property; in each country and each type of security there is some risk of poor title. Then again, even where the borrower is the legal and beneficial owner of the asset it does not always have the power to pledge it. There may be a restriction on its borrowing powers; where the lender is a foreign bank it may arise from exchange control regulations (less common than they used to be but still in force in some countries); or it may require the board of directors or shareholders to approve. While the bank's lawyers should ferret out these points, they can still sometimes trip up banks.

A bank can lose control of the asset even though title is perfect in every way. Most countries have some form of provision for reorganizing companies under court supervision but short of outright liquidation (Chapter 11 in the United States, Administration in the United Kingdom, Suspension de Pagos in Spain and so on). The powers given to the adminstrator (under whatever title) may include the right to sell the assets pledged, or to prevent the secured lender selling them. In some countries liquidation causes the immediate auction of all fixed assets, whether mortgaged or not.

Wherever assets are forcibly sold the secured lender can expect to receive the proceeds, and to be able to ensure a fair price. Nevertheless he loses the power to choose the time of sale and perhaps the chance of finding a buyer with a special interest who would pay more. This aspect may often cost him little or nothing; sometimes it may cost some incremental value of the security but not the major part of it. (At least this is so where the system is honest and efficient; a corrupt or incompetent procedure – and there are some – could cost rather more.)

Where the administrator can prevent the sale of the asset, the position is more variable. Banks need to know the rules in each country to judge the nature of the risk. As far as the present author knows, there is no country where the security is simply invalidated. But the rules as to how long – and why – an administrator can prevent sale, what responsibility he bears for loss of value and so on are different in each country. They may even differ depending on whether loss of value is due to passage of time or to usage, wear and tear and poor maintenance. Lenders to American railroads through equipment trusts often saw the value of their security eroded in this way.

In one sense this last point is more one of loss of value than of power to pledge. Loss of value more frequently relates to normal market valuc in the absence of disaster; it can also include loss, from accident or fraud, uninsured in error or because it was ininsurable. There are several broad categories of secured debt, and the risk of loss of value works differently for each.

The first is often called self liquidating; here the bank finances a specific transaction, the completion of which generates the funds to repay the loan. For instance, a bank may lend money to a commodity trader to pay for coffee from Brazil, and take a charge over the coffee; he may already have sold it at a firm price or may sell at a profit soon afterwards. As long as the sale goes as intended, the proceeds will repay the loan; the risk of loss of value arises only if the buyer defaults, or the seller fails to find a buyer at the price expected. Even then the bank will not normally lose money if the borrower is solvent, so that the value of the security is only the first line of defence. On the other hand a borrower who loses money in this way may do so more than once and may not be a very good source of repayment. Much the same comments apply if the transaction being financed is the purchase and sale of securities. Provided the bank knows the nature of the underlying deal, and makes sure its money is used for the purpose intended, the risk of loss is small; moreover, even if the worst happens, well chosen commodities or shares do not lose all their value overnight. Mostly they are traded on an exchange and can be quickly sold at a price close to the failed purchase price. In some cases the borrower must provide additional collateral, or margin, if the price falls. In all cases the bank has the right to sell the collateral immediately if its value drops below a stated level.

The risk is thus that the bank lends without being sure that the trade is truly self liquidating; that something goes wrong with what appears a sound sale; and that the price of the collateral falls before the bank can sell it. Banks nearly always lend less than the market value of the collateral to allow a margin of safety; how much less depends on the volatility of the price and the ease and speed with which the assets can be sold. Of course the bank also needs systems to recognize the need to sell promptly, and to implement the necessary decision fast.

The second type of secured lending may be called project lending, in a loose sense at least. Here the bank finances a specific project, a new factory or office block, or perhaps a bridge or the purchase of machinery. The end-product is pledged to the bank but is often not directly the source of repayment. For instance the factory may produce components; their sale generates cash which repays the debt. The factory itself is mortgaged to the lender, but its value is based on its ability to throw off cash. Failure to do so usually reduces the factory's value, sometimes severely. Equally an office building may be for the borrower's own use, or may be intended for letting to others. Either way it is the rental, actual or potential, which gives the building value; although the building may be sold and the proceeds used to repay the loan, the sale price derives largely from the rent level.

In a pure project loan, the bank will look only to the project and its cash flow to repay the loan. If the underlying assumptions prove wrong the project will lose value. In an extreme case it may become valueless and the bank lose the whole amount lent. For instance, if the price of oil drops sharply when an oil production platform is one-quarter finished, the expected cash flow may not make it worth while completing the platform, and all the money lent up to that point may be lost. Even when the platform is complete and operating it is possible, though less likely, for the price of oil to fall so far, or the cost of recovery to rise so far, that revenues no longer cover the operating costs. If the price stays low the platform may become worthless. The risk is greater in the North Sea than where capital and operating costs are lower.

In most cases the bank retains recourse to the company behind the project. Then the loss of value is not enough on its own to make loss certain; it depends on how important the project is to the strength of the company. Nevertheless at best the loss of value in the project weakens the overall credit, and at worst may wholly undermine it. Moreover the bank is most likely to secure itself when the borrower is not strong enough to carry it unsecured, and is therefore itself dependent on the success of the project. Legislation may threaten the value of a project by adding to its costs; lenders to the North Sea run a risk, if a remote one, of having to contribute to abandonment costs; recent American legislation threatens secured lenders with liability for cleaning up toxic wastes. Where the legislation comes into force during the life of the project it can be considered a form of lenders' liability.

There are specialized types of asset-based lending such as ship or aircraft finance, which are often not thought of as project finance. For the purposes of this discussion they are, even if of a special nature. The validity of the decision to lend depends on the lender's ability to judge the cash they will generate, and the impact on their capital value of a temporary, or more permanent, shortfall. The banks may also assess the airline or ship operator, but more for its competence as an operator than for its financial strength.

The third type of secured lending is general purpose. The security has no direct connection with the use of the loan; it simply provides additional support, usually because the borrower is a weak credit. The widest example is the fixed and floating charge in the United Kingdom, which covers all the borrower's assets. Other countries have broadly similar arrangements, although the details vary. The security here is not directly the source of repayment; if all goes well, this will be cash flow, or refinancing based on cash flow. The security is then a second way out; it does not ensure that the borrower remains solvent but merely that the secured lender receives more than other creditors if the borrower fails. Even here, though, the value of the assets depends on the borrower's ability to generate cash. Where he fails the assets will lose value, sometimes modestly, sometimes almost completely. In this case, the same reason that makes the bank want to realize its security may make it worth less to do so. Moreover to realize the security may put the company out of business; the decision to do this is fairly traumatic, and the bank may delay, while the assets lose value.

Finally, a third party may pledge assets not owned by the borrower, thus providing support in addition to his assets, rather than just giving the lender a preferred position. Here any loss of value will normally be entirely separate from the credit of the borrower, and genuinely gives a separate source of protection.

None of this is intended to argue against taking security in appropriate circumstances. The risk in security is, however, twofold; one is that it is not there when needed, for any of the reasons discussed. The other is that security is a misleading word; it gives a sense of safety that may be false. It is not always true that a borrower who has to give security is a weak credit, but it is true most of the time. A lender may take security without proper analysis of the risk or may fail to monitor the risk or to take prompt action when the credit begins to deteriorate. If the security then proves ephemeral he may end up losing more than if he had never thought he was secured. Then at least he would have taken the appropriate precautions for an unsecured credit, or not lent at all.

Finally, some types of lender's liability, discussed in an earlier section, are more likely to apply to security. For instance, the mortgagor of a building may be liable for taxes on the building or even for damages if part of it falls and hurts a passer-by. A holder of a floating charge who puts a receiver in may find that he is caught by a product liability suit and so on. None of these events is very likely, but all of them can happen in at least some countries unless due care is taken.

Senior debt normally has no secured debt ahead of it, and no debt which can claim any other form of preferential treatment. The risk therefore is first that this proves to be wrong, either at the time the loan is made or subsequently. In most countries it is fairly easy to check whether there is any secured debt at the time the bank makes a loan. It is not always so easy to be sure that the borrower never grants security to any other lender later. A negative pledge may put the borrower in breach of contract if it grants security, but need not invalidate the pledge or protect the bank if the borrower fails after giving it. Moreover not all negative pledges cover upstream guarantees; if two banks lend to a holding company, but only one obtains guarantees from its main operating subsidiaries, the other is in a weaker position in a liquidation. It may recover much less of its loan than the bank with the guarantees.

Senior debt does not often have subordinated debt behind it, but when it does the assumption is that the senior debt will be paid in full before the subordinated receives anything. However this assumption needs checking. Often the subordination only bites in liquidation; therefore by the time the senior lender really needs the benefit much of it may have been repaid; or he may find that to make sure this does not happen he must put the company into liquidation. This may not always seem the best way of recovering the debt from other points of view.

Even where the subordination applies before liquidation, it normally applies only to principal. Interest is payable unless there is a default on the senior debt. Interest on subordinated debt is usually higher than on senior debt, often much higher. Up to a point this is reasonable since the subordinated lender takes a greater risk; however, the interest is sometimes so high that part of it amounts to a return of capital. Indeed, from the senior lender's viewpoint, it may be worse than that; a true return of capital would at least reduce the remaining amount on which interest had to be paid. Exactly where interest ceases to be interest and becomes a return of capital depends on several things. If the risk is too high, however, it may be an equity risk; in which case the senior lender may wish to insist that the subordinated interest depend on the success of the operation, rather than being an automatic payment in all but the most disastrous situations.

Subordinated debt itself runs the highest risk of any form of debt.

Where its mere existence is not a sign of weakness, the risk of the borrower failing need be no greater than for any other debt. The main difference is what happens where there is failure. There is then a ranking; secured debt takes all the assets pledged to it, until it is paid in full, with any surplus of the pledged assets, and proceeds of all other assets, next being used to pay senior debt. Subordinated debt receives only anything left over. In some cases there are two or more layers of subordinated debt; then the junior subordinated debt receives nothing unless the senior subordinated debt is paid in full.

Again banks must watch out for concealed subordination. In Spain, for instance, there is a registration procedure. Registered debt is payable in the order of registration, and all unregistered debt is payable only when registered debt has been paid in full. Foreign lenders who are not familiar with the concept may be shocked to find themselves heavily subordinated.

In brief the risk that the borrower will collapse is not necessarily greater with subordinated debt than with senior debt; the risk of a total loss is much greater, as is the risk of a large loss when senior debt loses nothing.

Sometimes the existence of subordinated debt is a warning of financial difficulties. In restructuring of troubled companies, for instance, the only way to obtain needed new funds may be for existing creditors to accept a subordinate position; and in leveraged buy-outs and similar arrangements, there may be a layer or more of subordinated debt. This supplies support to the senior debt without the equity owners giving up a large interest, and is almost by definition a sign of high risk. (We should be careful to define what we mean by high risk, however; to a commercial banker, a bad debt ratio of one per cent is high. A two per cent risk on a loan is unacceptably high. Subordinated lenders may take a higher risk than that, but lenders in general will not make money if more than four or five per cent of the loans are lost.)

Indeed the holder of subordinated debt may increase the risk of loss by being too greedy; or by accepting such a weak credit that the fair return is too high for the borrower to service. In other words, while subordinated debt may have some of the functions of equity looked at from the senior position, this is less true when viewed from a junior position. Too much subordinated debt at too high a rate can be a factor in the final failure.

PUT NOT THY TRUST . . .

Banks also have to consider political risk in various forms. The most obvious is the risk of lending to a government which repudiates the debt. The second is the risk of cross-border lending, and the imposition by the borrower's government of a moratorium or, less drastically, exchange controls, which prevent a healthy borrower paying its debt. The third is the more general risk of poor economic management undermining a whole economy or industry; the fourth specific economic or other policies which hurt some companies (price controls or pollution requirements for instance); the fifth action aimed at supporting one company or industry which in practice is often at the expense of others, although the politicians fail to recognize this: subsidies which make an inefficient company competitive, and thus take away from the efficient the advantage they have earned; government monopolies which charge more than an economic price for essential supplies and thus make whole industries uncompetitive. The examples of this type of political risk are legion; they, and their effects, are also well enough known to be included under normal credit risks.

The more subtle risks arise where the lender relies on some form of government action – or inaction – to support the credit. This may be specific support for a particular company, based on a variant of the old refrain 'the government cannot afford to let this one go'; it may be based on past actions which have caused losses to the company which the government has chosen to recompense in some way. (Many government subsidies roughly offset the cost of other government actions. It can be fatal to assume that the government will never cut the subsidies without changing the damaging policies.) Or it may be because the company benefits from or even contributes to the success of policies which the government is not expected to change. And finally it may be based on some form of informal but morally binding (at least as the banks see it) obligation. There is also the oddity by which North Sea oil producers gain or suffer from the political decisions of OPEC, although no OPEC government has any jurisdiction over the North Sea.

One of the reasons why banks are too prone to believe in these various bases without careful analysis is that they have often done so successfully for many years. However there are several risks that banks need to focus on. The first is that governments rarely do these things with the aim of helping the banks; the desire to help industry is only fractionally stronger. They do them because they fit whatever the government's aim may be at the time – most often, in a democracy at least, having a close if not always obvious connection with getting re-elected. Thus, if the government's view of how to achieve its end or the end itself changes, so will its policies; the question of who gets hurt is likely to be secondary. This means that even the longest-standing policies can change in ways which banks have come to accept as unthinkable. This has been a particular danger since the advent of economic policies which believe in letting the market decide; desirable as these are in many ways, they have changed the whole approach of many governments to what they will support or why; and to what subsidies, direct or hidden, they will continue.

The second reason is that government's views of moral obligation and indeed of ethics are very different from those of business. This is always true but particularly where there is any sort of intragovernmental dispute. Most governments take the view that, since they represent the national interest, little things like breach of their word have less importance than they do in commercial life. When this basic view has the passion of a power struggle added to it, industry and banks are ill-advised to get in the way, or to rely on the outcome meeting their expectations.

The most dangerous situations of all seem to arise in countries which follow the American pattern of independent arms of government; even the United States can behave like a banana republic if Congress feels the Administration is encroaching on its prerogatives, or vice versa.

5 Trading and Related Risk

GLOSSARY

Currency swap An arrangement under which two parties exchange payments of principal and interest in different currencies. For example, Bank A might swap ten-year fixed rate dollars for either fixed or floating rate sterling. Both sides pay interest throughout the life of the swap and exchange principal payments at maturity; some currency swaps also start with an exchange of principal, others do not.

Floating rate notes (FRN) A type of bond where interest is payable at
fixed intervals above a marker rate. The most common rate is six-month LIBOR, but a wide range of other maturities and markers is possible.

In the money When an option or similar instrument would give a profit if exercised, it is in the money. When the price of the underlying asset is below the level necessary, it is out of the money.

Interest rate swap An arrangement where parties exchange interest payments, calculated on a notional principal which does not change hands. The interest is in the same currency, but on a different basis; the most common is fixed against six-month LIBOR, but there are many varieties; they include the so-called basis swap where parties exchange floating rates calculated on two different markers. These might be LIBOR versus US commercial paper rates, three-month LIBOR versus six-month or more complex combinations.

Off balance sheet An asset or potential asset which in its present form does not appear on the balance sheet, but which could do so if a specific event occurred. For instance, an unused commitment will generate an asset on the balance sheet when it is used; a guarantee, if called, will give rise to an asset, often of dubious value.

Standby commitment A commitment by a bank to lend, issue a letter of credit and so on in conditions where the client does not expect to use it often, if at all. Examples include commitments to support ratings for commercial paper; rating agencies require these so that companies can always pay maturing commercial paper. In practice, neither side expects that the borrower will be unable to raise commercial paper without some prior warning.

Yield curve The different levels of interest rate for different time periods (such as one month, three months). Usually interest rates get higher the longer the period they cover. Sometimes the difference is small (a flat or shallow yield curve), sometimes it is large (a steep yield curve). Sometimes, short-term rates are actually higher than long-term (a reverse yield curve).

Warrant A negotiable piece of paper, often issued with a bond or equity issue, entitling the holder to buy a given security at a given price. Most often the security is issued by the company issuing the warrant, but not always; a commodity warrant entitles the holder to buy the commodity instead of securities.

TRADING RISK

Trading risk results from a position in a particular type of asset or flow of funds. The position can arise for a number of reasons, some of which are discussed below under the following headings: market making risk, underwriting risk, investment risk and hedging risk. However banks and others take pure trading risk in their day to day business.

Interest rates are one of the main elements in trading risk. There are several ways in which banks take interest rate risk, and several different types of risk they take. The first is the simple risk on an unmatched loan or deposit. A bank may lend money for six months; if it matches it with a six month deposit, there is no trading risk (except perhaps of an opportunity loss if it turns out the bank could have made more money by leaving the loan unmatched). Often, however, the bank will make a larger immediate profit by funding the loan with very short-term deposits, perhaps at call or at one week's notice. These funds may be cheaper than the six month deposit, giving the bank an immediate spread between the cost of funds and the earnings on the loan. Or it may choose to take a fixed deposit for an intermediate period, perhaps one month. With a steep yield curve, this will lock in a spread for the period of the deposit; if interest rates have fallen by the time the deposit matures, the bank can lock in a still larger spread for the remaining life of the loan. If it took the wrong view interest rates must still rise sharply before the loss in the remaining five months will wipe out the profit of the first one. (Or the bank can take in a six month deposit but lend it initially for one or three months. This would imply the opposite view of interest movements or yield curve to the first operation.)

Which of these the bank does will depend on the yield curve and the bank's view of which way rates are likely to move. A steep yield curve allows the opportunity to take a large spread initially, but often indicates that the market expects that there will be a change. It may expect longer-term rates to fall; if they do funding short at first gives the chance to lock in a higher spread later. Or it may believe that short-term rates are about to rise, in which case it may be more profitable to match fund and lock in the spread while it is still available.

Either way (and these are only the simpler possibilities) the trader has profit opportunities and risk of loss from two sources. One is the absolute level of interest and the other is the yield curve. In either case, the risk is from an unforeseen change; a profit may come either from the existing yield curve or from sound judgement of changes.

A bank also runs a trading risk when it buys an instrument, such as a bond or FRN, the price of which is largely a reflection of interest rates. With a FRN the interest in question is usually for six months, although some have a shorter interest period; with a fixed rate bond it can be anywhere from a year to 30 years, although banks usually trade in the shorter maturities. Bonds give the same opportunity to play the yield curve as with a deposit but over a longer timescale. The bank may for instance buy a five year bond and fund it with a one or two year deposit, rather than one or two months. The difference between a bond or FRN and a deposit, however, is that the bank can sell the former. Lower interest rates may enable the bank to fund the bond more cheaply, but will also increase its price, giving the bank the option of selling for a capital gain. Or the bank may expect rates to fall and buy to obtain the resulting capital gain.

The risk is the opposite of the opportunities described above. Whenever the bank takes an unmatched position, or buys an asset hoping to sell at a profit, it runs the risk of losing money if it judges wrongly. Sometimes it can offset movements in interest rates and capital value in whole or in part; at other times it will lose both interest and capital.

FRNs carry two types of interest risk which affect the capital value differently. Take a normal FRN with a six month interest setting, bought at the start of an interest period; the bank may fund it in any of the ways already described for a deposit. If it chooses a three month deposit, and interest rates move up sharply, it may be unable to fund the remaining three months at a profit, and find the capital value of the FRN has fallen. However, because the rate will be reset in another three months, at the then market rate, the capital loss will be small and temporary. But FRN rates are set in line with a benchmark interest rate; in the euromarkets this is usually LIBOR. A bank may buy an FRN at, say, one-quarter per cent over LIBOR; if the market decides later that the right margin for that issue is one-half per cent over LIBOR, that will cause a loss of capital value related to the final maturity of the FRN; the longer the remaining life the greater the initial loss and the longer before there is any significant recovery. The bank will also hold an asset yielding one-quarter per cent less than it could get in the market if its funds were not committed. If both the interest rates and the margin move against the bank it may have a loss in the three months until the resetting, followed by a smaller but longer-lasting loss from the higher margin.

There are many other instruments based on interest rates. They include forward rate agreements, swaps, options, warrants and futures in interest rates or in assets whose value reflects interest rates. There are caps, floors or collars which provide protection against movements above or below an agreed level in interest rates or above one and below another. Some of these are used as much to hedge against trading risks as they are to trade; nevertheless, whatever the intent, each instrument considered in isolation creates both a profit opportunity and a risk of loss. Sometimes the profit or loss is income, sometimes capital gains, often a mixture of the two. One side of the risk for some of these may be a premium paid, and lost, if the interest rates do not move in the direction feared and hedged against.

Of course they are rarely considered in isolation. A bank, particularly a large one, will trade one or several portfolios rather than one or two individual transactions. It may choose to run open positions, partly mismatched positions, or positions in one instrument which are offset by contrary positions in other instruments. In practice it will often run a complicated mix of these and other combinations which are well beyond a lending banker's understanding. But the basic point remains; to the extent that it tries to make profits, whether on income account or capital account, by taking positions which expect a particular type of movement (or lack of it) in either interest rates or the yield curve or both, a bank takes a trading risk.

Much the same comments apply to exchange rates. A bank can buy dollars now for sterling and hold them for appreciation against sterling; in that case it will be able to buy more sterling for the same amount of dollars and show a profit in sterling terms. Or it can do a forward exchange contract, agreeing to pay one currency for another at a date in the future, but at a rate set now rather than when the exchange takes place. If the actual rate moves in the bank's favour it can make a profit by later buying forward, for the same maturity, the currency it has sold, or by waiting until the contract matures and buying spot. Or it can match at the time it enters the original contract, making no profit except commission but insuring itself against loss.

As with interest rates the bank can also use bonds, FRNs and so on to buy a foreign currency asset which will appreciate if the currency does so, but yield it perhaps more interest than a deposit. Or it can do a long-dated currency swap, buy futures, options, currency warrants and so on. Again, in some cases, it may pay a premium which it only recovers if the currency moves enough to put the option, for example, 'in the money'.

Currency trades also involve interest risk in the two currencies. This may be direct or indirect. For instance, if a bank buys dollars for sterling as in the original example, it will earn interest on the dollars at a dollar rate instead of in sterling at sterling rates. If the dollar rates are higher or lower than sterling rates this will affect the cost to the bank of the transaction and either add to or reduce the loss if exchange rates move against the deal. Since buying dollars forward against sterling enables the bank to earn sterling interest instead of dollar, the forward exchange rate will normally reflect the difference between the rates. The reverse is also true, at least in a free market; if the market's view is that the relative strength of two currencies differs from that suggested by the interest differential, then the interest rates in one or other currency will move, unless the spot rates move first. Put another way, a change in demand for one currency over the other can be accommodated by a move in two out of the three indicators, or in all three, but not in one only. Equally, if the government or market believe that interest rates in one currency are wrong, and cause them to move, then one or more of three things must happen; either the interest rates in other currencies move in the same direction, spot rates move or forward rates do. The theory of arbitrage behind these points is well known. The point is that it makes the trading risks more complex to assess, since traders cannot be sure which factor will cause which movement.

Bonds or other tradable instruments also have elements of both currency and interest risk, at least where the bond is in anything other than the buyer's native currency. If a sterling-based investor buys dollar bonds, a change in dollar interest rates will affect the dollar value of the bond; it is also likely to change the sterling value of the dollar. These two changes may tend to offset or to reinforce each other. For instance, if the dollar weakens against the pound for reasons of general economic policy, the US authorities may raise interest rates to defend the dollar against further weakness. The sterling holder then loses both because the dollar is weaker and because the value of the bond in dollars declines as interest rates rise. Or the US authorities may raise interest rates to keep control of the domestic money supply; this may impress markets, and the dollar may strengthen, thus at least partly offsetting the decline in the dollar value of the bond. Moreover it is rarely clear whether a currency is weak or strong because of economic fundamentals, because its interest rates are out of line with its main competitors or for other reasons; nor is it clear how long one factor, such as interest rates, will continue to be the main force behind moves in exchange rates; nor why or when markets will begin to pay more attention to a new factor pushing in another direction.

The relationship between the various factors in a free market are theoretically fairly well understood. Converting the theory to practice, however, is hindered by the constant tendency of governments to interfere. This may take the form of exchange controls, of intervention in interest rates or exchange rates directly or through things like quotas or tariffs. Whatever the nature of the action, and however well other benefits may justify it, it complicates the life of a trader and adds to the risks he bears.

The same type of description could be applied to trading in bullion or other commodities. This section, however, is not a trading manual; the author is wholly unqualified to write such a manual. It is intended to illustrate the main types of trading risks which traders assess in deciding which risks to take and which to avoid. They are, however, not the only risks which affect the profit or loss on trading activities. Some other risks are really subdivisions of trading risk, or special forms of it, and experienced traders are as aware of, and experienced in dealing with them, as they are with the main trading risks.

Others, however, are less obvious; some occur in nearly all trading, others in all of a particular broad category, others only infrequently. They all carry a risk in addition to their particular characteristic, that of being overlooked. They may then spoil a sound trading decision, turning what ought to be a profit into a loss (or much less often the reverse). When this happens traders may claim it was pure bad luck, something nobody could have foreseen; or they may try to blame somebody else. It may be bad luck as far as the individual trader is concerned; that depends on what type of support and training his employer gives. It is not bad luck for the bank as a whole. It may be the result of taking a view; sometimes the cost of protecting against a risk (or of increasing the level of protection) is greater than the benefit. The bank may then argue that, for the portfolio as a whole, the losses are a normal cost of doing business. As long as the portfolio earns enough the cost is acceptable. This can be perfectly sound risk management, provided the bank correctly judges the risk/cost relationship and watches for changes in it. In other cases, where the bank has made no conscious decision to accept the risk rather than the cost, the loss is pure bad management.

These risks include market making, hedging and liquidity risk, operational risk, credit risk in several forms, settlement risk and documentation risk; sometimes underwriting risk; and, in a growing number of cases, insider information or conflict of interest risk. Tax risk is less common, but can apply.

MARKET MAKING RISK

In normal trading, the trader has complete freedom to decide what to buy and sell and when, what to hold for how long, and when simply to be out of the market altogether. A market maker is in a different position. The exact rules, and their formality and enforceability, depend on the market concerned, but the basic thrust is always the same. The market maker undertakes to make a two-way market at all times; in other words he will quote a price at which he will buy and one at which he will sell, at any time and without knowing whether the enquirer wishes to buy or sell. The market maker can thus at any time find he has taken a position, long or short, which is against his basic view of the market. In markets which are moving fast or which suddenly lack liquidity, this position can become quite large quite fast, and be difficult to unwind except at a large loss.

Of course there are ways in which a market maker can limit this risk in times of crisis. He can widen the spread between the bid and offer rate. This may help when the movement is reasonably well controlled or where there is a genuine two-way business, even though the weight of interest is on one side. By making its price on that side less attractive and on the other more, he can hope to balance the weight of interest. This will hardly work, however, in a market collapse or buying panic. Then the investors' concern, and that of other market makers trying to square their own position, is to cover at whatever price they can. Market makers can also quote for smaller than usual amounts in bad times; for instance a normal quote might be for $10mn; in a one-way market, the quote might be for $1mn. And there are various forms of hedging mechanism which the market maker can use to offset all or part of the involuntary risk, although these in turn may be less available when they are most needed, as a number of people found in the crash of October 1987. Finally, in a telephone market, though not in one where deals are done face to face, the market maker can fail to answer his telephone. This is not correct behaviour, and nobody admits to doing it; many people complain that others have done it.

Whatever the protections, it takes skill and knowledge to know when to use them, which to use and how much. To use too little, too late, or the wrong one may cost money or damage client relationships and reputation in the market. To use none may give a reputation for courage, or foolhardiness, and can cost large amounts. In an extreme case it can erode such a large proportion of capital that the firm cannot continue in business. On the other hand, to run away from the risk may carry formal sanctions, and certainly will tend to undermine the market's confidence. Where market making is only one of a number of services the resulting loss of business in other areas may be painful.

UNDERWRITING RISK

There are two main types of underwriting discussed in this section, which does not cover either insurance underwriting, or the underwriting of NIFs and so on; these are more akin to a commitment or a form of insurance than to true underwriting. Securities underwriting is the commitment by one or more firms to buy an issue of securities at a given price. The securities are usually newly issued, and the underwriting is part of the process of distributing them to a wider range of investors. In other words, although the underwriter commits to take the issue, it is a bridging commitment; he expects to be able to sell them at an immediate profit. In some systems the underwriter actually buys the securities and sells them on immediately; in others the managers of the issue undertake the selling effort, and the underwriters only buy if nobody else will.

There are variations between systems as to how far in advance the underwriter is committed and at what price. Some systems concentrate the risk, some disperse it more widely, perhaps by a sub underwriting. But these differences are secondary. They affect the specific incidence of the risk on particular houses but not the underlying principles.

The main risk here is of failure to sell the issue, so that the commitment unexpectedly has to be met. There are broadly three reasons why this can happen. The lead underwriters may have misjudged the market in general, or the more specific market acceptance of the issuer. Or general market factors (most frequently interest or exchange rates) may change between the date of commitment and the date of issue. Thirdly, the market's view of the issuer may change, perhaps owing to new information, often about credit. Whatever the precise cause, the result is that the underwriter is left holding securities it did not expect or want to hold (at least in most cases; where the system disperses the underwriting risk, some underwriters may be natural holders, underwriting to earn a little extra for doing what they wanted to do anyway).

The underwriter then faces several types of risk. If the cost of carrying the position is greater than the income from the securities, he has a running loss, or carrying cost. This risk does not hit every failed underwriting; where there is a steep yield curve it may be quite profitable, for a while, to fund the position short. The yield curve may also indicate that the market expects rates to fall, in which case the underwriter may fairly quickly be able to sell the securities at an acceptable price.

In other situations, however, the yield curve may have shifted, or may continue to shift, against the underwriter, so that as the carrying cost gets greater so does the loss on the capital value of the security. This indeed is the second risk; the failure to sell the issue at the original price means that its market value is less than the underwriter's purchase price. He must in most countries mark to market and report this loss; he will in any event have a realized loss if he sells immediately. To hold in the hope of recovery runs the risk of a continuing carrying cost, and in the end an even larger capital loss.

There is also the risk, greatest where the underwriting risk is concentrated, that the issue will be virtually impossible to sell, sometimes at all, sometimes in size. Unless the underwriting judgement was unusually bad, this should be only a temporary position, but the price may have to drop substantially before it corrects itself. Even then it may only be possible to sell small amounts without pushing the price sharply further down and adding to the loss.

The lead underwriter may have an additional risk, in that he may feel obliged to 'stabilize' the issue. This is in effect making a market without adjusting the price to reflect supply and demand. While it risks creating a false market, and is frowned on in some quarters, there are respectable arguments in favour. They revolve round the need to avoid prejudicing the issue while the market, and potential investors in particular, familiarize themselves with it. Whatever the arguments, it is a widely followed practice, and clearly involves the lead underwriter in some risk. He may be able to lay this risk off on other underwriters, but this in turn carries a risk to his future business. If the cost of stabilization is too great, he may have difficulty in bringing underwriters into future deals. This will either prejudice his ability to do the deals at all or force him to take a larger share of the risk than he might otherwise choose to do. The lead underwriter also normally acts as market maker for the issue; in a growing number of markets he is obliged to do so. The commitment to underwrite, therefore, is often also a commitment to make a market and take those risks.

Underwriting also involves credit risk. First, there is settlement risk. The underwriter who actually buys the issue has to pay the issuer, get the securities, deliver them to the end seller and get his money. In many cases, this is arranged through a clearing house such as Euroclear, and the risk is small. If the underwriter ends up holding the issue this mechanism will not apply to the eventual sale, which will carry whatever form of settlement risk applies to the issue.

More important is the risk on the issuer itself, which applies to all debt instruments. (Some would argue that this is not true when the issuer is a government issuing in its own currency. The counter argument is that, while a government always can pay debts in its own currency, by printing more money, it is not certain that it always will; in particular it is not certain that a successor government, perhaps after a revolution or major change in constitution, will do so. In most cases this risk is small, but it exists.)

The issuer risk has several stages. First, a decline in credit standing may cause the issue to fail, leaving the underwriter with the risks discussed above; secondly, a decline may make it harder to sell when the issue fails for other reasons; thirdly, there is the risk that the issuer's credit collapses completely, leading to default and bankruptcy. In theory, if the underwriter has performed due diligence adequately, this risk should be very small in the early stages. The longer the underwriter has to hold the security the greater this risk becomes, even where the due diligence was well done.

There is strong evidence that the level of due diligence is not as high in most markets as it should be. This both adds to the credit risk directly, and creates a risk of its own, even where the initial underwriting succeeds. The issuer may fail within the first several years of the life of the issue. Investors may then claim their money back from the underwriter on the grounds that he knew or should have known about the weakness that causes the collapse. Unless the underwriter can show that he had checked with 'due diligence' (an American term which has become widely used), he may find himself liable to recoup the investors' losses. At one time this risk would have been serious in the United States only; more countries are introducing, or have introduced, similar laws, spreading the risk more widely than is often recognized.

As far as the author knows, there have been some issues where the bank voluntarily repurchased an issue, but none in the euromarkets where underwriters were held liable for lack of due diligence. Most lawyers in the field would add a qualifying 'yet' to that statement. Some City solicitors have even considered withdrawing from eurobond documentation, through fear that poor due diligence would undermine the basic assumptions underlying their legal opinions.

Apart from the due diligence risk, lead underwriters run risks relating to the documentation of the issue. These include any breach of the laws on prospectuses, risk of damages for misrepresentation and so on. In some ways they are similar risks to those run by the agent to a syndicated loan; however, in most countries the securities laws are fiercer than banking laws.

The second type of underwriting is of loans. A bank or group of banks may agree to raise a given amount of finance on given terms. Both sides know that the banks expect to find others to share in the finance or perhaps take all of it; if that expectation is wrong, however, the banks commit to provide it themselves. They may actually lend before syndicating, or they may merely guarantee the availability of the money well before the borrower needs it, thus giving themselves time to arrange a syndicate or other vehicle.

Whatever the exact mechanics and timing, the principle is the same. The risks are broadly similar to those in underwriting a bond issue, but details differ. For one thing the underwriting period is longer, and documentation less standard. Even in a successful syndication, there will be a period of weeks, sometimes months, before the underwriters know how much they have to keep themselves. Even when other banks agree in principle, it is almost always 'subject to documentation'. It is unusual, but by no means unknown, for a bank to withdraw on these grounds. Moreover, if the underwriters have been out-negotiated, they may find documentation a sticking-point with potential participants.

Apart from the risk of misjudging the initial terms completely, this slower process gives more chance for conditions to change before the syndication is complete. In theory, once a bank has said yes in principle to terms, it should not back away because conditions change; but obviously the temptation to reject marginal points increases.

The other aspect of risk is that if the underwriting fails the underwriters are left with an even less liquid piece of paper than with a failed bond. Although the growth in loan sales means that some loans prove saleable even after a failed syndication, banks cannot count on this. The risk of a failed underwriting leaving a permanent holding of the underwritten paper is thus greater with a loan than with a bond.

INVESTMENT RISK

Investment risk combines some of the risks of lending and trading, arguably reducing both. Investment in the context of this section excludes equity investment; it applies to the purchase of bonds and similar instruments with a view to holding rather than trading. The investor need not intend to hold until maturity, although in practice with the shorter instruments that often happens. But the intention to hold for a time means that the credit risk is in some ways similar to that of a loan; certainly the longer life means that there is more time for things to go wrong. There are some qualifications to this similarity. On the plus side most investments can be sold, although the ease of sale, and certainty of a fair price, varies widely with the investment. Moreover, within whatever limits the market places on each investment, it will always be easier to sell at a full price – or to sell at all – if the investor is alert and sells before the market generally is aware of the decline. On the other hand, a bank investor who does business with the issuer must always be alert to the insider information risk (see below). Then again, while this is perhaps a weakening tendency, it is probably still true that borrowers are more reluctant to default on public issues than on private bank loans.

Against this, the investor cannot expect to exercise the same degree of control over the issuer that a bank can – though the bank does not always do so. Indeed the investor may often find that the documentation of his loan gives him little or no power even to ask for information. The lack of a trustee, and its impact on the ability to co-ordinate a response in times of trouble, has already been discussed. This may be another aspect of underwriting risk, as well as a risk for the holder. It is arguable, although many banks would disagree, that the lead underwriter has a responsibility to the investors. After all, it was he who underwrote on terms which left them unrepresented in a crisis.

Finally of course investment risk includes settlement risk; if the investor sells before maturity, he settles with a counterparty; if he holds to maturity, he still runs the risk of surrendering the bond, not getting paid and not being able to prove he surrendered it. This last risk should be small, and there should be provisions in the indenture to cover it; they may not, however, protect against an inefficient or defaulting trustee, nor against genuine loss of the bond in the settlement process. However small the risk may seem, it is only so because there are tested methods of avoiding it. An investor who is not aware of the risk can hardly assure himself that the documents protect him.

In summary, the main investment risks are a form of credit risk, but with some variations from the risk in an otherwise comparable loan. On one side there is the liquidity and the hope that the bonds may be better treated than bank debt in case of trouble. On the other side are the often weaker documentation and the possible inability to co-ordinate a response.

HEDGING RISK

Banks and other companies hedge to reduce or avoid risk. Sometimes the hedge takes the form of a directly matching transaction; for instance, a bank may do a five-year interest rate swap, paying fixed dollars against floating, and shortly afterwards do one the other way for the same notional principal and maturity, but perhaps receiving a higher fixed rate than it was paying, or paying a lower margin over LIBOR.

The word 'hedge', however, is more commonly used to mean a different transaction which nevertheless provides cover. A bank with a swap under which it pays fixed dollars and receives floating may hedge by taking a floating rate deposit and using it to buy US Treasuries. The idea may be that the bond has the same maturity as the swap and that it is an indirect method of matching. More often the bank intends to wait for fixed interest rates to rise and then match the swap with a higher fixed rate. However if rates drop instead the bank could suffer a heavy loss if unhedged; hedged with a Treasury, it can sell for a capital gain that largely offsets the loss on the interest flows.

Other hedges use futures or options against an outright risk; or one currency to hedge a risk in another which is expected to move in line with it. (For example, a bank with a major risk in Dutch florins might hedge it in Deutschmarks because the DM market is more liquid, and the florin is closely tied to the DM in the European Monetary System.) There are many possible examples, some of which can be very complicated and involve several different transactions to achieve the desired result, but these examples should make the basic point.

Distinctively hedging risk takes two main forms. These are the risk that the hedge disappears, and the risk that it turns out to be invalid or at least incomplete. The first is primarily a credit risk, either on a counterparty or on a clearing house. If the counterparty to a swap defaults, then the value of that swap as a hedge is lost. Similarly with any form of option unless it is traded on an exchange, or cleared through a clearing house, which guarantees performance; even that leaves a clearing risk. Even a loan which is not paid leaves the bank open to the cost of the funding deposit and the risk that the cost will increase.

The second hedging risk is that the transaction used as a hedge does not precisely mirror the one it is hedging, and either provides no protection or, more probably, partial protection only. For instance, in the examples given above, the Treasury bill rate may not move in precisely the same way as the fixed rate available in the swap market. The bank may therefore lose part of what it thought it had hedged. This risk is greater in countries where the government bond market is thin. There may be no bond which exactly matches the maturity of the swap, and the closest may be a thin market which moves erratically, and which would certainly move against the bank if it tried to sell a large amount quickly.

A risk which to some extent combines the two is that a hedge may not be available when needed. For instance, some hedging strategies require the hedger to buy cover only if the market moves against it to a certain extent. When the need arises the relevant market may be closed, illiquid or otherwise unavailable, perhaps for credit reasons.

There are other risks which apply in some cases, but they arise out of the transaction needed to perfect the hedge; they are not hedging risks in the true sense. For instance, many forms of hedge may involve settlement risk, either in all cases or in those where the hedge is activated. Others may involve documentation or operating risk and so on.

THE INTERACTION WITH CREDIT RISK

In a sense, all the risks discussed so far in this chapter are subdivisions of trading risk. Credit risk affects all of them, in several ways. One is the same as for a loan, at least up to a point, but there are some important differences.

The risk of insolvency, or of default or restructuring to avoid it, is broadly the same for all holders of debt, whether it is a non-transferable bank loan or a bond quoted on many stock exchanges. There may be a difference of degree, but not of kind, where borrowers continue to pay interest on their bonds after they cease to do so on bank loans. But where they default the loss is the same on both.

An important difference is the ability to sell a bond. With an investment holding this may be a fall-back position; with a trading position it is a major reason for buying. In either case the ability to sell is a factor in the decision to buy and particularly in the credit decision that the paper represents acceptable risk. If the credit decision is wrong, the impact may be that the paper is temporarily, or perhaps permanently, unsaleable; equally, however, the result of a wrong trading or investment position may be that the protection against credit risk is reduced or eliminated. The latter point is covered in more detail under illiquidity risk, below.

In practice the impact of a wrong credit decision on a bond holding is not usually a complete and permanent inability to sell; sometimes it is a temporary inability, more often only a drop in the price at which it can be sold, and sometimes in the amount that can be sold quickly without pushing the price even lower. If the credit error is a major one the position may deteriorate rapidly to one where no sale is possible, but more often this takes months or even years. The holder will have the chance to sell at a loss rather than accept a complete default.

This type of credit loss can also happen where the basic credit judgement is sound. Take an extreme example. A bank has a choice between making a five-year loan to an AAA rated company, or buying a five-year bond from the same name; it judges that the risk of complete default is vanishingly small. It chooses the bond, for non-credit reasons; after two years it wants to sell the bond, also for non-credit reasons. However in the meantime the issuer has been downgraded by the rating agencies to AA and the market fears that it will soon be further downgraded to A. The bank therefore sells the bond at a considerable loss. Its basic credit judgement is proved right and the issuer pays the full interest and principal on the bond when due.

Credit risk in a trading or even investing sense thus has a broader meaning than when making a loan. It requires a judgement not merely of the actual ability to pay when due, but of anything that threatens that ability, however slightly. Indeed, anything that even seems a threat may affect the value of bonds and other tradeable paper.

The question which credit men have to ask and answer for trading and investment holdings are therefore more sharply focused than when lending. As well as 'will the borrower repay?', which remains relevant, they must ask:

(1) Is the issuer subject to any volatile factors out of its control? might these damage its ability to pay, or seem to the market to do so? A positive answer might relate to the price of a key raw material, for instance copper. Even though the bank's analysis may show that the company can easily survive any normal fluctuation, the market may be inclined to cut the price of its securities when copper prices rise. (Note the word 'may'; the market may equally have taken the copper price risk into account. It is a credit judgement whether the price of copper is a major or minor factor in the company's survival, or how far it has to move before it changes from a minor to a major factor. It is a market judgement as to the stage at which the bond price will move. The best trading judgement will accurately assess both the credit risk and the market's reaction to that risk; it will then relate the two to see whether there are any anomalies of which it can take advantage, or the effect of which it should avoid.)

(2) Even though we do not expect the company to fail, how likely is it to suffer some loss of credit quality? The price of a bond will reflect the credit quality from time to time, regardless of the

final outcome. A bank's traditional credit analysis may be wrongly directed, and never ask the question; or it may answer it wrongly. Either way, the cost of a mistake is greater than if it had done the same level of analysis for a loan. The cost is also relatively greater if the bond is bought purely for trading than when bought as an investment. With an investment, after all, it is not certain that the bank will want to sell; even if it does it still has the option of holding to maturity. Where the bond is a trading asset, however, the sole purpose of buying is to sell at a profit. There can be nothing worse for a trader than to buy a bond on an interest view, have that view proved right but still lose money because the credit view was wrong and the loss from that mistake more than matched the profit on the interest movement.

(3) How far could our company suffer from contagious credit doubts? If competing companies lose credit quality, will the market impute the same weakening to our company? and will the market be right, or does our company manage its business to protect itself from the risks? Banks also need to consider country and political risk in a similar context. A sound company in a weak country may still meet its debts in full, but if the market begins to fear that the country will reschedule its external debts, the bond price will fall. Equally, if a government changes the rules on a company (price controls, subsidies, higher interest rates or other costs, pollution controls and so on), it need not break the company but may hit the bond price.

In summary, the relationship of credit to traded instruments is more short-term, more based on perception and less concerned with the absolute failure of the borrower/issuer than in a loan. Broadly the same point is true with underwriting, except that if the original decision overlooks a short-term credit risk it may leave the underwriter with a much greater risk position and credit exposure than expected.

The relationship to other types of trading risk is slightly different. As discussed in earlier chapters, the credit risk is in a sense a contingent one. With a forward exchange contract or swap, for instance, the risk is that the counterparty fails, and leaves the bank with a different trading position from the one it expected. The bank only loses money if the position it originally took was well judged; if it was not the failure of the counterparty could in theory leave it with a profit instead of a loss, although in practice this is not likely. Where the forward contract or swap was intended to hedge another position, the position is now unhedged, but again this will only cost the bank money if it turns out to have needed the hedge.

Even with a familiar loan and deposit, there is an element of trading risk as well as the obvious credit risk. If a bank makes a six-month loan and matches it with a six-month deposit, it takes a view of the likely movement of interest rates in relation to the yield curve over the six months. If the borrower defaults after, say, two months, the main loss is the principal; but a secondary loss is the interest. The size of the interest loss in that six months is the interest that it has to pay on the deposit; if interest rates have fallen the loss is greater than it would have been if the bank had taken a two-month deposit. Thereafter it will have to continue to pay interest on a replacement deposit, and will be exposed to changes in interest rates. Since it will have no asset to repay the deposit, or to earn interest which it can use to service the deposit interest, a higher or lower rate will directly affect the running cost of the loss. Eventually it will in effect have to pay the deposit from capital; this again will cost it the earnings it could have made by lending the capital. Ultimately this loss will be offset by lower dividends and share value, so that the shareholder pays.

ILLIQUIDITY RISK

The traditional bank loan was illiquid, in the sense that there was no prospect of selling it before maturity; banks ensured liquidity partly by managing the maturity profile of their loan portfolio, partly by holding a liquid reserve of cash and money market assets, partly by controlling the maturity of their liabilities.

In today's conditions there is a range of liquidity in a bank's credit-related assets. This starts with the illiquid loans already mentioned; works through a negotiated market for medium-term loans and swaps, with complex documentation, short-term loan sales, still negotiated but often under a master agreement which makes each deal easy to complete, and finally the traded instruments such as FRNs, bonds, warrants and some commercial paper. Here there is an active market with quotations on computer screens, market makers and at least a theoretical ability to buy and sell with a telephone call at any time.

The main benefits of liquidity, and therefore the main risks of illiquidity, relate to trading, return and balance sheet management. These are vitally important factors, but are not the main focus of this book. However, a brief summary is necessary, since these factors interlock with the credit decision. In trading, liquidity is essential to allow the bank to take large positions without moving the market and to unwind them. This may either be to take a profit, or to avoid a (further) loss if the original view has proved wrong. The same is true of balance sheet management; banks may be willing to underwrite large positions which do not fit their balance sheet strategy, but only if they are confident that the position is a temporary one. Thirdly, a bank may accept a low return on an asset, if it believes the market will accept a yet lower one, so that it can sell at a profit.

Liquidity changes the view of credit risk in several ways. First, a bank may be willing to take a larger exposure if it expects to be able to reduce it quickly by selling into a liquid market. Secondly, even if it does not initially intend to do that, it may be easier to accept a low return. For instance, a bank might be offered a five-year floating rate loan at one-eighth per cent over LIBOR, with the rate reset every three months. Viewed as a short-term asset, the margin may be quite attractive for a strong borrower. Committing the bank to that rate for five years may be less attractive. The ability to sell the loan if the bank thinks that margins are likely to rise may make it easier to take the risk.

The other side is that liquidity may make it easier to accept a weaker loan structure. If a bank is locked into a loan for five years, it will need more protection than if it can sell the loan at any time. Of course whoever buys it ought to need the protection, since as long as the loan is outstanding someone will be at risk. Nevertheless, at least in the euromarkets, it is broadly true that the credit protection built into the documentation for a liquid asset is less than for an illiquid one. Sometimes the market is more relaxed about the credit risk because it is liquid, sometimes it merely wants the non-credit advantages and ignores the credit price.

The main risk therefore is that the investor gives up too much credit protection for the advantages of liquidity, and then finds that the liquidity is illusory. Illiquidity in this sense comes in three main ranges. The market may be either permanently or temporarily thinner than expected. This will mean that investors can only sell a few units at a time: if several want to sell at the same time, the price will drop quite sharply, for instance from 100 to 97; in trading terms this is a big loss. A commercial bank beginning to wonder whether the issuer would ever be able to service the bond, however, might find it a small price to avoid the greater risk.

The second level of illiquidity is where the market temporarily seizes up altogether. This may relate to the particular issuer; if a bond rated by a major agency is put on credit watch, for instance, it may be impossible to sell until the agency announces whether it will downgrade the issue, since there is no basis of information for judging the right price. Or there may be a wider problem, as when a city, country or industry is seen to be in trouble. All connected issuers may become illiquid until the market can judge whether the problem can be solved and how it affects each issuer. An investor who believes the damage will be severe may be unable to sell quickly, before the price drops as other people reach the same conclusion. Or, as with perpetual FRNs in late 1986, there may be a sudden change in the market's acceptance of an instrument. Whatever the precise reason for the temporary loss of liquidity, it prevents the investor from selling when he wants to, whether to avoid the result of a sharp decline in quality or for other reasons.

Even more serious is the situation when the market seizes up permanently or for such a long time that it amounts to the same thing. Here the bank is locked into an illiquid loan, but at a rate and with a level of protection appropriate to a liquid one.

MISMATCH RISK

A mismatch risk arises when a bank deliberately lends long and borrows short. This primarily creates the trading risk described earlier in the chapter, which results from a change in interest rates with funds remaining freely available at the new price. The mismatch risk describes a change, in market conditions or in the bank's own standing, which threatens to prevent the bank obtaining funds at all.

If a bank cannot get funds because of doubts about its own status, this suggests a more serious problem than just the mismatch risk. Still, a heavily mismatched book can aggravate the problem, while a closely matched one can make it slightly more manageable. To take an extreme example, a bank may lend heavily in six months and cover mainly with call money. A crisis in its credit will then be harder to deal with than if it had lent only out to three months and matched all loans exactly. In the latter case it would have greater flexibility to run down its book while retaining a matched position; if it had to renew some of the loans as they matured, it would still be going to the market for relatively small and infrequent amounts and for periods which make sense. With the heavily mismatched book the bank has a difficult choice when it realizes it faces a problem. If it continues to fund very short, that will mean it is constantly approaching the market for money at a time when the market is wary of its name. The very short funding may make the market even more suspicious, particularly if the bank is known to have a mainly long asset book – and the market quickly senses these points. And while banks are reluctant to cut their lines to a troubled bank too abruptly for fear of rocking the boat, they will often try to cut back gradually. The more often the troubled bank has to approach the market, the more chances it gives others to make a series of small cuts in its facilities. On the other hand, if it tries to match the six-month loans by taking large six-month deposits, the market may be unwilling to lend for that long. Any premium over the market rate to recognize the bank's suspect status will be greater for six months than for shorter periods.

Where the difficulty is with the market generally rather than with a particular bank, this in turn is likely to be worse the longer the period of mismatch. In the larger markets and in normal times, there is little difference in the availability of one-, three-, six- or twelve-month deposits. When markets get tighter, the worst impact is almost always felt at the longer term. Depending on the market and how serious the position is, it may become virtually impossible to get one year money while six month is available only at a high rate and in small amounts. Or it may be the six months that is unavailable and the three months that is expensive and hard to get.

In one sense the mismatch risk is one which other banks and regulators as well as the bank allowing the mismatch should beware of. From the regulator's point of view, a heavy mismatch can be a cause of difficulty; a sign of mismanagement which may have implications for the quality of management of other areas; and a serious impediment to any attempt to rescue the bank discreetly. From other lenders' point of view it is a warning of possible trouble, and that the regulators may require other banks to help bail the weak bank out.

None of this is to argue against the careful use of mismatching as a trading technique. It does argue however that banks must be aware of the possible impact on their own credit, and avoid mismatch positions extreme enough to worry the market. It also suggests that mismatching is a technique for the strong; a weak bank can afford to take much less risk in this as in other areas.

ALL SWINGS, NO ROUNDABOUTS RISK

Insurance of availability of funds has long been one aspect of banking. Examples range from the unused overdraft, through the committed acceptance line and the revolving commitment. A new form of insurance has entered the market in the last few years. Under it banks provide a standby facility to be used only when other, normally cheaper, facilities are not available, sometimes at all, sometimes below a certain price. Typical examples are standby facilities backing commercial paper lines and commitments under NIFs, RUFs, MOFs and so on. In all of these the borrower expects to be able to borrow more cheaply from another source than from a normal bank loan. In each case the other source is short-term with no commitment; it has every incentive to stop lending if it becomes even faintly concerned about the borrower's credit or if interest rates for this type of loan become less competitive.

The bank will receive a facility or commitment fee for the standby, and a margin over LIBOR or another benchmark if it actually lends. The borrower will, however, want to keep the fee as low as possible. It is in a sense an additional cost of the cheaper borrowing; if it is too high the borrowing ceases to be cheap. The borrower will also want to keep the cost of using the facility low, although where confident that he will rarely if ever use it he may generously concede a higher rate to obtain the lower fee.

The bank then has a facility which may never be used and which will almost certainly not be used in normal, let alone favourable, conditions. It will be used either because the market has taken fright about the borrower's credit or because the market is no longer prepared to lend to this quality of borrower at this rate. In other words the bank will only lend at the committed margin when that margin is below what it could get in an uncommitted position, or when if given a choice it would not lend at all. What the bank loses on the swings of this type of usage, it will have no chance to recover on the roundabouts of profitable usage.

This poses an interesting question about pricing. The borrower will prefer to make any unavoidable concessions on the margin, since he does not expect to pay it, and knows that if he does pay it will look cheap at the time. He will try to keep the commitment or facility fee low, because he expects to pay that. For the same reason the bank will want a higher fee; it will also be reluctant to see the margin too low, because that will make it more likely to be used and more painful if it is.

The new capital adequacy rules discussed in Chapter 8 will make the cost to the banks of this type of commitment more obvious. They may therefore help to solve the pricing question, but they do not change the underlying problem. That is always there, and should not need regulators to point it out.

INSIDER TRADING/CONFLICT OF INTEREST RISK

As outlined in the opening chapter, this book does not deal with fraud or self-inflicted risks of similar nature. However there are two types of risk which arise out of the insider trading possibilities which are not self-inflicted. The first is the restriction which inside information causes. For a start a bank may not use inside information to buy or sell securities. But how does a major bank with worldwide operations know whether it has inside information somewhere in the bank? Part of the answer is that the bank may not use the information to make the decision, but may make the decision through someone who does not know about it. But how does a bank prove that it did not use the information? If a bank as adviser to a company receives information in one unit, the initial assumption will be that it knows that information in other units. If it buys or sells a security at a better price than is possible once the news is public, a plea of ignorance will attract some scepticism. Banks establish Chinese walls to cover this risk, but it is still hard to prove a negative.

One method is known as the 'Grey List'. Here anybody in a firm or bank who has inside information advises a central point. A limited number of senior people have access to this list, which is checked before an investment purchase or sale. This check is only part of the approval process, and if approval is withheld, the trader does not know whether the reason is Grey List or something else. Also the trader will go through a central point to get credit approval (if the bank is a commercial one where the source is likely to be the account officer) or will go to a credit officer. Either way he should never have direct access to the person who is likely to know too much. In this as in much else, the aim is to avoid actual insider dealing and any appearance of it, however unjustified.

Equally, at the time a name goes on the Grey List, someone must check whether the bank is trading in securities of that issuer, or taking other action which causes problems; if so, someone must decide whether to cease trading. Part of the problem is that banks cannot just tell the trader 'sorry, you cannot deal'. This warns immediately that something is happening, and thus in effect gives him the inside information you are trying to protect. Even worse, for a market maker or active trader in the company's securities to stop trading for no apparent reason tells the market there is something happening. Thus there may be a conflict: on the one hand the only safe thing to do is to stop trading; on the other, to do so may involve a breach of trust to the client.

However sophisticated its controls, there is thus always the possibility of a bank dealing in good faith but seeming to use inside information. The opposite risk probably worries commercial bankers more than investment banks. This is the possibility of being unable to use independent judgement because of inside information. Take a simple example. Bank A buys the bond of a AAA rated issuer. Two or three years later the people responsible for the holding come to the conclusion that the issuer is deteriorating and is likely to lose its AAA rating; they therefore decide to sell, but first check the Grey List through the normal channel, and are told they cannot sell. Their analysis was based on public information, but because a colleague has inside information which proves them to be correct they cannot act on the judgement.

Investment banks have lived with these risks for years and, at least in the United States, have developed rules to deal with them. These rules probably do not eliminate the risk entirely but they reduce it to manageable levels and, banks hope, ensure a sympathetic hearing from the authorities if something slips through the net. Commercial banks are finding it harder, for two reasons. One is that until recently they did not deal in traded assets, the price of which is sensitive to such information. They therefore do not have a long tradition of such systems. The other is that a commercial bank tends to have broader and deeper relations with its clients, and a key point about those relationships in the past has been their value to banks in protecting their credit exposure. Now this key aspect is the source of the fears about insider trading, so that the problem is more than one of setting up a system. It requires the banks to change their whole approach to approving credit, and in some cases to change long-held philosophies about the way to follow a credit risk.

The final risk is to worry so much about these risks that the bank ends up refusing good business where there is no insider risk.

Part III

Risk in Instruments

6 Loans and Loan Substitutes

GLOSSARY

Deep discount A bond or other instrument with a nominal interest rate well below the market rate, which is sold at a discount from par. The actual interest paid, plus the present value of the capital gain when the bond matures and is redeemed at par, approximate a normal yield. The method has tax advantages in some jurisdictions, or may be more attractive to a borrower which expects a low cash flow to improve over time.

Due diligence In origin, the process by which share and bond underwriters in the United States satisfy themselves that the issuer has disclosed all the relevant facts in its prospectus. More generally the need for a bank to satisfy itself that it fully understands the borrower/issuer.

Market maker A bank or securities house that undertakes to buy and sell a security at any time in reasonable size; it will quote both bid and offer prices without knowing which side the other party wants to take.

Multiple option facility (MOF) Similar to either a NIF or a RUF (see below), except that the borrower can use several different instruments, not just one. In London, for instance, the instruments might include sterling and dollar acceptances, euronotes and straightforward advances.

Note issuance facility (NIF) A facility under which a borrower can issue notes in an agreed currency and range of maturities. A group of banks, known as the tender panel, will bid for the notes, but within a maximum limit. If the tender panel fails to bid for all the notes the borrower wants to issue, a group of underwriting banks must lend at a predetermined spread over, usually, LIBOR.

Revolving underwriting facility (RUF) Similar to a NIF, except that RUFs are an investment banking facility; instead of the tender panel, the investment bank leading the deal, or sometimes several, act as dealers for the notes and find buyers in that capacity.

Zero coupon bond Similar to a deep discount bond except that no interest is paid; the whole yield comes from the capital appreciation at maturity.

TRADITIONAL LOANS

The main risks on traditional loans are described in the first section proper of Chapter 4 (on the risk of a loan or direct credit). There are, however, a number of variations which banks need to keep in mind. These are mostly of emphasis – some risks are more important in some types of lending than in others – but in a few cases additional risks apply. Some of these are inherent to the types of lending, others arise from mistakes which, however well known they ought to be, still occur.

For instance, overdrafts and some other types of short-term lending are 'payable on demand'. In some countries that means exactly what it says, but in most it is more or less heavily qualified, depending on the banking law concerned. In the United Kingdom, for example, the courts require 'reasonable' notice before cancellation of an overdraft. They will decide what is reasonable in each case, but the notice should allow the borrower to meet obligations entered into in good faith in reliance on the overdraft. Where the overdraft is used for short-term working capital, it may be enough if the borrower has time to clear any cheques issued before the notice was received, while others might need several months' notice. Many other countries take broadly the same approach. In some countries the mention of a date in the letter establishing the facility may commit the bank to lend until then.

Whatever the exact rules, there are two risks. First, to rely on being able to demand without checking the rules may leave the bank unable to recover its debt as fast as expected. In some cases this may add to the loss. Secondly, to cancel a facility without a clear right to do so may cost more than the amount of the loan or overdraft. The action may bankrupt the company, laying the bank open to a suit for damages from the borrower and other creditors. Even if the company survives, it may suffer severe damage for which the bank may be liable.

This is also one of the cases where what might be called 'the summary judgment risk' is possible. Sometimes a bank's best chance of recovering its money is to get a quick judgment which allows it to attach assets, sell security or make some other specific move. In most countries the only hope of doing this is to apply for summary judgment; it exists in some form in almost all countries although under a variety of names. Since many countries have a time-lag of several months to several years before a normal case comes to court, summary judgment may be the only form of action fast enough to help. The courts will give it only if the borrower offers no defence, or one that is so weak that the court rules there is no case to try.

In these cases, borrowers often try desperately to find a defence. It does not have to be one which will hold up, only one that will cause the judge to send the case to full trial. In some countries – Spain, for instance – there are also very precise formalities which must be met; any breach, however slight, will entail loss of the right to summary judgment. Once this is lost, the delays before full trial and the possibilities of further delaying tactics put great pressure on the banks to settle. Moreover, in many jurisdictions, judges are hostile to banks, or there are nationalistic pressures to support a local borrower against a foreign bank; or one of a number of reasons why a judge may prefer to avoid giving summary judgment.

Borrowers under overdrafts therefore may claim that a bank officer promised that the bank would not call the overdraft until the project was finished; or deny that the bank warned that it might cancel the facility; or falsely claim that the bank knew that it was needed to finance a contract. Equally guarantors may claim that they were not given the legal advice to which 'innocent' borrowers were entitled. (In one case a highly sophisticated Chinese family, which had given guarantees to half a dozen banks, and boasted of its financial expertise, used this ploy with at least partial success.) Or they may claim that they were never told the exact details of the facilities, or that these were different from the terms of the guarantee; or that the attempts made by the bank to recover the maximum amount from the borrower, thus reducing the amount due under the guarantee, were in some way fraudulently aimed at diverting assets at the guarantors' expense. Where the loan was financing a project, they may claim that the project was intended to be the sole source of repayment, and the borrower never expected to pay it from his general resources.

Such claims are rarely true, but are often difficult to disprove. In summary judgment the onus is on the bank to show that there is no case to answer. Unless the bank has kept the most meticulous records of everything said and done, this sort of negative is very hard to prove. Even with meticulous records the bank may simply not have foreseen the type of point, and may therefore not have covered it. It is not normal for a bank to go around proving that it is honest in everything it does, after all. Normally this is taken for granted by both sides. And of course where the case does come to full trial, the onus is then on the borrower to prove that the bank undermined the basic contract, rather than on the bank to prove that it did not.

These points can sometimes override even the most careful documentation. But apart from them there are variations of documentation risk in different types of loans. Where the documentation is a simple one-page letter, as with an overdraft or other short-term line, the risk is small. A more complicated and longer-term agreement is more likely to contain areas which can be misinterpreted or for some reason do not work. And facilities which contain complex options are more likely to be misdrafted by lawyers who do not understand the way in which the transaction is supposed to work and therefore find it hard to express it clearly.

A straightforward unsecured loan does not normally involve settlement risk; the borrower either pays or he does not. Some forms of secured loan do, however, although sometimes indirectly. For example, banks sometimes finance the settlement of securities or commodities sales. To make the payment but fail to receive the asset, or vice versa, costs their customer money, perhaps enough to make him insolvent, in which case the loss becomes the bank's. Or the bank may fail to prove that a solvent borrower accepted responsibility for the settlement process, and that the bank followed procedure correctly; it may suffer either documentary risk or operating risk. Banks which lend against self liquidating security may run a more direct settlement risk. They may make loans to enable borrowers to pay for an asset which then becomes their collateral; this is common in the securities and commodity industries. If the loan is paid over to a seller who does not deliver, the bank then has an unsecured loan to a borrower who has just suffered a loss, perhaps a crippling one. Equally when the loan comes due for repayment, the bank may need to release the asset to obtain the funds. In each of these cases there are two additional risks: either that the documentation fails to allocate the risk for a system failure clearly (documentation); or that the bank mishandles the settlement, and is therefore liable to the customer for the loss (operating).

DEPOSITS AND REDEPOSITS

Deposits with a bank are in essence a form of loan, and the depositor takes a credit risk; redeposits simply involve one bank depositing with another. The main lending risks thus apply in principle to all deposits. In practice, however, there are some differences. Because deposits with a bank are the main store of value for many customers, bank deposits are more sensitive politically than most loans. In some countries this leads to various forms of protection, mostly aimed at small depositors; for instance, the Federal Deposit Insurance Corporation (FDIC) in the United States insures small deposits up to $100 000. Because of the cost of meeting all such deposits for a failed bank, there is real pressure on the FDIC to rescue banks before they actually fail, and thus protect even large depositors. Other countries have various types of guarantee fund or other means of covering depositors. Some of them cover only the first 75–90 per cent of deposits, so as to retain some incentive on the depositor to choose a secure bank.

One of the risks associated with deposit insurance and the more general difficulty of letting a bank fail is called moral hazard. This is the risk that because all banks are protected, depositors and other creditors will cease to worry about whether a particular bank is sound, and put their money where they can get the highest return regardless of risk; they think there is no risk because of the protection. Or the bank's management may think the same and take risks which are disproportionate to the return on offer. The latter is only likely directly where the bank is already in serious trouble; it is easy to play double or quits with the government's money. For a still solvent bank the risk is that management does not get the warning signals from loss of business that might prevent it going over the edge.

Redeposits are the main way in which banks take this type of risk. In many ways they are no different from any other loan. Nevertheless, because banks lend to each other in much larger amounts than they normally lend to companies, there is the extra risk of a domino effect. The failure of one bank may cause a spreading series of failures. Or the failure may drag the depositing bank into a forced rescue, where it loses some of the flexibility it has with a company. Although there are political and other pressures on banks to support failing companies, they are less than with the failure of a large bank.

BONDS AND FRNS

Bonds and FRNs carry several types of risk, although they may be borne by different parties. To distribute bonds to the market, underwriters carry underwriting risk, and at least some of them also carry market making risk. Once the paper is out of the primary underwriting period, there may be other market makers as well; also normal traders, taking normal trading risk in the instrument. Holders will either take trading risk or investment risk, depending on why they hold them, and all parties to purchase or sale will take settlement risk, and sometimes clearing house risk.

All holders face credit risk, and the various documentary risks that go with it. It is not always clear how this is divided between various holders but it is always there. If the bond is truly liquid the loss may be borne in small parts by a range of holders. A buyer at par may become concerned, or may become aware of market concern, at an early stage, and sell at, say, 97. The buyer at 97 may later sell at 94 as the problems become more apparent, and so on until eventually the bond formally defaults and the issuer is declared insolvent. The holder at this time may have paid about 45, and will lose the difference between that and the pay-out in liquidation, or whatever he has to give away to negotiate a cheaper restructuring. A successful restructuring may allow the bond to recover to something close to its full face value; some liquidations pay out more than expected, more even than the closing purchase price of the bond before suspension. Or a temporary weakening in the issuer's credit may be reversed, so that those who sold at a low price in effect give a profit to the buyers. In other words, a phantom or overestimated credit risk can cause losses as well as a real credit risk.

It may not be easy to tell how much of the loss is due to credit risk, how much to other factors. For instance the buyer of a bond at 100 who sells it at 97 may think the whole of the loss is due to a change in the interest rate climate. It may take careful analysis to show that in fact the general market decline only accounted for part of the fall; if the issuer's credit is more dependent on low interest rates than most, it may fall further when interest rises than the rate change alone justifies. Or the issuer may suffer for reasons unconnected to interest rates but which coincide with the changed climate.

Because of this diffusion of risk, and because most holders will see liquidity as a defence, it is easy to overlook the importance of credit risk to bondholders. Whatever the situation for any one holder, as a group they face the same credit risk as a single lender. They may indeed suffer a greater risk if the documentation gives less protection, as discussed in earlier chapters.

Where there is a trustee for the bondholders, this may reduce the risk due to loss of control, but the trustee faces certain risks. If he reacts too soon or too strongly to potential problems, he may lay himself open to a claim for damages from the issuer; if he leaves it too late, he may face irate bondholders. In practice most trustees will have a fairly broad middle path they can follow, so this risk is not very great. A trustee who does not check the documentation carefully may find that the path has been dangerously narrowed. Equally a bondholder risks loss if the trustee is deficient. While some failures may make the trustee liable for negligence, there are broad areas where it is a matter of opinion what is sound judgement; in these areas it is difficult to prove negligence, and often unfair even to claim it.

Paying agents will be faced with a form of settlement risk. They will need to make payments of interest, frequently, and of principal less often. It used to be common for issuers to deposit the funds the day before the agent was due to pay. More recently issuers have chosen to save a day's interest by paying the funds to the paying agent on the same day. Even where the paying agent's base currency is the one being used, it may be difficult to ensure that the outgoing payments reach their destination the same day, unless the agent gives irrevocable instructions before the money is due from the issuer. If the money does not then arrive, the agent will at least know within a few hours and can take prompt steps to recover the funds.

Where the agent is in Europe, but the payment is in US dollars, the agent will not know of any failure to pay until, at the earliest, the following day; if there is a weekend or a holiday involved, he may not know for several days. He will of course have a claim against the issuer for the money, and if that fails may be able to reclaim it from the bondholders, depending on the wording of the paying agency agreement. In most cases of non-payment, the reason is an administrative mistake, and the agent recovers the funds, but there is always the risk of credit problems and a permanent loss.

The issuer also faces some risks with bonds. One is a trading risk; with a fixed-rate bond he runs the risk that interest rates will decline, and he will pay too much. This is usually acceptable, since the fixed rate protects against the opposite risk of a rise in rates. At the time of the issue the borrower presumably thinks either that such a rise is more likely than a decline, or that the risk is greater in other ways. With an FRN, the issuer's trading risk is the other way round; he gains if interest rates fall and loses if they rise. In addition he takes a basis risk. If he issues at, say, 25 basis points over LIBOR and later finds he could issue for 10 over, that 15 basis point difference is a cost throughout the life of the issue, regardless of what happens to LIBOR itself.

The issuer runs a risk, too, on the underwriters and paying agent. He delivers the bonds either against payment or before payment is received and the underwriters deliver them on immediately to the final buyers. If the payment chain fails for any reason the issuer may still be liable on the bonds even though he has not received the money, or has received only part of it. Equally, if he deposits funds with a paying agent which does not pass them on to bondholders, he may have to pay twice. In practice of course both these risks are recognized and minimized or eliminated in the standard procedures and documentation. Nevertheless they are risks of which the issuer should beware if only to avoid them.

The issuer faces other risks on the lead underwriter in its capacity as adviser. He risks paying too much, either because the timing of the issue is wrong or because its terms give more to the investor to ensure a success in light of what the market expects at the time of issue. Or if he aims for too favourable terms, he risks a failure which leaves him without the money, or paying more for it because he has had to raise the yield to offset the initial failure. Or he may gain a reputation for being too greedy, which may increase the cost of his next issue.

The decisions on these points are the issuer's, and therefore he carries the ultimate responsibility for the risk. And if his underlying philosophy is too greedy or short-sighted, there is often little an adviser can do to convince him that the basic approach is wrong. Few issuers, however, have great familiarity with the market; they must therefore rely on advisers to give them the advice on timing and on terms, and to indicate what are the relative costs where an issuer has conflicting aims. For instance, the balance between the desire to pay as little as possible and to retain a high-calibre group of underwriters on terms which the market thinks fair is clearly delicate.

The more important risks the issuer takes relate to terms other than price – the credit terms. (These points apply in only slightly modified form to syndicated loan agreements as well.) For instance, a borrower/issuer who agrees to ratio covenants which are too tight runs the risk of being in default when there is no real increase in risk to the lender/holder. The risk exists with a bank loan, whether syndicated or not. However generally speaking the banks will not call the loan where a too tight covenant is breached in a way which does not threaten ultimate repayment. They may of course extract a little extra from the borrower to pay for the breach, but unless they believe it is serious they will not try to accelerate repayment, with all the risks to the borrower that involves. The same may prove to be true with bonds, but it is much harder to predict what a wide range of holders will do. The issuer also depends on the trustee, if there is one, to handle a crisis in the best way. While the trustee's duty is clearly to the bondholders, their interests often, probably mostly, coincide with those of the issuer. After all they want their money back; the company wants to survive, and can only be sure to do so if it repays its debts.

Nevertheless it may be difficult to get a coherent response, particularly with bearer bonds, from widely scattered individual bondholders. Unless there is a competent trustee, and unless the document gives him appropriate powers to take some initiative, it can be impossible to get the bondholders to take a constructive approach to the problem. This is one reason why borrowers are more reluctant to default on bonds than on bank loans. The banks may go along with this reluctance where the bond issue is a small part of total debt. The cost of a failed rescue may be greater than the cost of allowing the borrower to pay interest on the bonds, even though this interest is then not available to meet the other debts. Where bond issues are a large part of the total, or where there is a default threatened on principal rather than interest, the equation may be less favourable. And where the rescue calls for new money banks will be most reluctant to provide it to pay interest or principal on bonds whose holders contribute nothing. While banks might not expect bondholders to participate in new money, they would hardly agree to provide it themselves unless the bondholders contributed in some way. Thus the bond documentation should allow the trustee, where there is one, to participate in discussions leading to rescue proposals. Only then can he be an effective link between the banks, the borrower and the bondholders, with some chance of reaching a compromise that is acceptable to all parties. Lacking a trustee, a provision allowing a vote on a proposal is even more crucial. And in either case the voting requirements should allow a binding vote without being able to identify all the holders.

Failing appropriate provisions on these lines the issuer risks being unable to arrange a rescue even when there is a fair chance of success. All companies risk ultimate failure and liquidation; there is no need to add to the risk unnecessarily.

NIFs, RUFs AND MOFs

NIFs, RUFs and MOFs share a key characteristic, although the details differ. They are underwritten at a maximum margin above a marker (say, 10 basis points over LIBOR), or in the case of a MOF, several markers. If the borrower can borrow below that maximum through a dealer or tender panel, he does so; if not, he borrows from the underwriters at an agreed spread. This may be the maximum, and may be over the same marker, but need not be. Still, the cost will rarely be attractive to the borrower.

Underwriting banks take the all swings, no roundabouts risk. The borrower will always use the most attractive option. In normal conditions this will be to draw under the tender panel facility. Only if something unexpected happens will he use the underwritten facility. The something may be specific to the borrower, which usually means that his credit is weakening; it may relate to a group of which the borrower is a part, which either affects the borrower's own credit or makes the market think it has; or it may be a general change in market conditions. Whatever the reason, the underwriting bank only lends at a time or rate, or both, which is unattractive to it. The borrower may borrow at times when the bank would like to lend, but only from the bank if it is low bidder on the tender panel. This may be acceptable if the bank is receiving a large enough fee to compensate for the risk, but in the 1980s competition usually prevented this.

The overall risk of NIFs and the rest is greater than that attached to just one facility. If the market moves banks which have underwritten many NIFs may suddenly have a much larger balance sheet than they expected. This risk may be less damaging than it used to be; the proposed capital adequacy rules will ensure that most banks keep at least some capital against unused commitments. However, the proposals are for 10 to 50 per cent weightings, depending on maturity. Thus usage will require more capital even under the new regulations; only the size of the increase will be smaller. Banks which are already undercapitalized for their outstandings risk being overwhelmed by such a change in the market. Even banks that are better capitalized could find the sudden surge of usage embarrassing.

To make it worse, the surge may come at a time of general concern about credit standards; or it may follow a change in the market's view of a large category of borrowers, perhaps in a particular industry, country or other region. Whatever the exact reason, the bank risks being seen to expand its balance sheet just when the market thinks it should not, and doing so by putting on assets the market considers suspect. The impact on the bank's market standing and ability to raise funds cheaply, or in extreme cases at all, could be severe.

There are other risks peculiar to NIFs and the rest, though some aspects are shared with loan sales, discussed below. When the borrower is in trouble they can make a modest problem more serious than it would otherwise be or make a serious one harder to handle than with a conventional loan. The nature of these facilities gives parties conflicting interests in trying to shift the risk from one to another. Take a simple NIF where the borrower begins to run into trouble during a six-month drawing period. The underwriting banks may face a difficult decision. Do they look for an event of default, even a purely technical one, to justify them in refusing to lend at the end of the six months? Where there is a clear-cut event of default do they accelerate? If they do either of these things they risk aggravating the problem and perhaps pushing into liquidation a company which under traditional lending methods they would have worked to save, with a good chance of success. If they do not, they risk having to lend to a deteriorating borrower and perhaps accept substantial losses which they could have avoided. The risk is thus that banks lose their main incentive to work with a troubled borrower.

There have been no publicized cases of NIF borrowers in difficulties. The instrument and all the variants are relatively new and have faced only boom times. There undoubtedly will be such questions asked and answered in the future, but in mid-1988 we have no precedents on which to draw. There are reasons why banks might not accelerate, even where on the facts of the NIF alone that might appear the sound reaction. Some will have substantial other exposure to the borrower, so that the damage done by a premature acceleration would be greater than any saving on the NIF exposure. One protection for the borrower is have NIFs and the rest underwritten only by banks which have a profitable relation with it and other exposure. Or banks might fear to set a precedent if they themselves buy paper from NIFs underwritten by other banks. Or, if they are not close relationship banks, they may only become aware of the problem a short time before the end of the six months and fail to analyse the situation fast enough to take such a major decision in time. However this can work the other way; a bank which is not sure whether the difficulty is serious might choose to play safe.

The banks' attitude could also depend on the nature of the default. It would be harder to accelerate on a material adverse change clause than on a specific and clearly identified breach of a covenant. However much discretion the material adverse change clause gives to the bank, it can only be a matter of opinion. The bank lays itself open to possible suits for damages unless it has a cast iron case that the company has weakened so far that its ability to pay is threatened. If the case is that strong it will almost certainly have broken more objective tests – if such tests are in the agreement.

This introduces a risk of conflict in negotiating the documentation, which may weaken the limited discipline banks are able to apply to borrowers. Where banks are lending direct, without any third party, they have an interest in negotiating ratio and other covenants to protect them if the borrower weakens. Although many borrowers resist this interest, the more intelligent recognize that well designed covenants have value for them as well. Some wish to resist but do not have the strength to do so in a straight lending situation. In a NIF, they can argue that they have a duty to the potential buyers of the paper not to undermine the strength of the underwriting commitment; more credibly, that if the covenants are too tight, the banks will not be able to sell the paper where there is even the first sign of trouble and thus will find themselves lending in unattractive conditions even more often than now. Or at least they would be able to argue this if the buyers of paper paid any attention to the terms of the underwriting agreement and thus the protection it provides. In mid-1988 there is no evidence that they do, but again this may change when a NIF borrower runs into difficulty.

The holder risks seeing the trouble too late to obtain repayment before the underwriting banks can refuse to lend. This risk is greater the tighter the covenants in the underwriting agreement, but also depends to some extent on the nature of the borrower. Some borrowers can change much more quickly than others; this is partly a question of size but also of concentration of market or of raw material cost, to mention only a few factors. A buyer of NIF paper who does not take the trouble to identify the type of company issuing it is more likely to face a credit loss.

The conflict between lenders as to who is at risk, and the danger of inexperienced lenders obstructing a rescue, may lead to an issuer's unnecessary failure. This risk also applies to all who are unable to pass it to someone else. A borrower in trouble is most likely to recover if it has the support of its banks and other lenders. Banks are really the only lenders used to giving this support, and even they give it best when they have a close relationship with the borrower and trust in its management. The underwritten NIF does not require that, although it does not preclude it either. Some companies support relationships with their banks as much with a NIF as with other facilities. But since one of the advantages of NIFs is their low price, the tendency in the 1980s has been to award NIFs to banks on price rather than on knowledge of the borrower. In this case banks may try to duck out of responsibility for a rescue as described above. If they succeed the buyers of the paper are left as the main lenders and are likely to be ill-qualified to run a rescue. Even where some bank lenders stay in and take a lead they may not be close to the borrower and thus may not be the best banks to do the job. They certainly risk finding it much harder to whip the non-bank lenders into line. In particular, if the borrower needs new money as part of the rescue, buyers of paper who thought they were taking a short-term risk will rarely agree to lend more and be locked in for several years.

Issuers also take a risk with NIFs, which applies to all undrawn commitments. The underwriter may be unable to meet their commitment to lend when called upon. It is at least arguable that the extra risks NIFs put on a bank add to the issuer's risk.

In brief, NIFs, RUFs and MOFs, despite their undeniable advantages, carry a variety of risks for all parties to them. They have only been available for a relatively short time, and there have as yet been no failures to show how serious these risks are in practice. The answer will probably be that the risks are like most other lending risks. They will be manageable for banks which take them seriously and guard against them as far as possible. They will be painful and possibly fatal for banks which underestimate them.

ZERO COUPON AND DEEP DISCOUNTED BONDS

The point about both of these is that interest is paid only at maturity. In the case of zeros, this is true of the whole amount of interest; for deep discount only of the difference between the nominal rate and the market rate.

The mechanism is the same as when a bank discounts a bill of exchange. The borrower issues a bond with a face value of, say, $1000. However, because it is paying a below-market rate of interest – or no interest with a zero – the issuer receives less than the full face value. The actual amount is calculated to give the original purchaser the same percentage return if he holds it to maturity as if he had lent in a conventional way and received a market rate of simple interest. A purchaser who pays $800 for a $1000 bond will receive $200 more at maturity than he paid initially. The present value of that $200 is equal to the present value of a stream of payments of *x* per cent per annum over *y* years when *x* is the current market rate and *y* is the original maturity at the time of issue.

Apart from tax risks, which vary from country to country, the main risks for zeros and deep discounts are the same as for other bonds. Because of their specialized nature, however, their liquidity is more open to question than with conventional bonds of comparable credit quality. Two extra risks, however, are more directly due to their character, and are greater the longer the life of the bond. One is the delay in payment and concentration of the whole amount (or larger part of it with a deep discount) at the final maturity. With a conventional ten-year bond paying interest annually the holder receives nine payments of interest and one of principal and interest combined. If the issuer runs into trouble half-way through the life of the bond, at least he will have paid four or five instalments of interest first. Moreover each payment is relatively small and the consequences of not making it painful, so that he will try hard to make the sixth and subsequent payments. Equally, if he only runs into difficulties a short time before maturity, the final payment will be principal and only one year's interest. This will be large compared with interest alone, but much smaller than the amount which would be due under a zero or deep discount.

With a zero nothing is paid until maturity. With the example given above, of an original $800 leading to a repayment of $1000 the extra amount is not very large. In some cases the maturity might be as long as 15 or 20 years; in a high interest environment the original amount received might be $200 rather than $800. The risk of failure during this long a period is significant, and if it occurs the lender may get nothing back. Even if a troubled borrower struggles on to the final maturity the size of the payment may then be more than it can handle. The same point is valid for a deep discount bond, but to a lesser extent. At least some interest is payable, even if not a full market rate; the loss caused by a failure half-way through the life of the bond is greater than with a conventional bond but less than with a zero.

The risk of fraud is greater with a zero. With a normal or deep discount bond interest is payable regularly. A bearer bond has coupons attached to it which must be presented for each interest payment. If the bond is forged, there are thus repeated opportunities during the life of the bond to discover the forgery or other fraud; plainly the temptation to forge a bond which will probably only be checked once is greater. The longer the delay before the forgery is discovered the harder it is to identify the culprit, and the more likely he is to get off scot-free.

A zero swap gives similar problems, by adding to the swap, in effect, a series of loans of shortening length and the same final maturity. The cost of the credit risk on these loans, and on the unused commitment until they are drawn, is added to the final payment and thus to the credit risk.

SYNTHETIC ASSETS

Synthetic assets result from combining a financial asset with a hedging instrument such as a swap, to transform the nature of the asset for the investor. In a fairly simple, and also fairly common, example a bank buys a fixed rate bond although it wants a floating rate asset. It swaps the fixed income on the bond into floating and uses the swap income to service the underlying deposit. It thus ends up in the same approximate position as if it had bought a floating rate note; not in exactly the same position, because the purpose is to improve the return. (The process works equally well where a bank buys FRNs and swaps into fixed.)

Of course the swap need not be interest rate, or not only; a bank may swap fixed yen bonds into either fixed or floating dollars, for instance. Nor need the process apply to a single bond; some of the most successful synthetic assets result from repackaging bond issues that have not done well in their original form. The investor who did not like Ruritanian dollar fixed rate bonds at 50 basis points over Treasuries may buy them in their new form of floating rate sterling notes at 35 bp over LIBOR. Unlike the bank purchase of a synthetic asset outlined above, this may represent a loss to the underwriting banks who were left with the original issue. However it limits and in some cases reduces the loss, and enables the underwriter to move an illiquid asset off its books.

The holder of a synthetic asset thus has two sets of risks, those attached to the bond or FRN, and those attached to the swap. Taken separately they are no different from those on any other bond or swap. Together, however, they raise one or two points. For instance, if the bond defaults there are different possibilities depending on the form of synthetic asset. If it is as in the first example above, the bank which holds the bond loses its interest (and principal, if that is swapped). Apart from the cash loss it also has an uncovered swap, with the trading risks discussed in Chapter 5. If the swap fails, it still receives its payments on the bond, and its loss is whatever trading loss it has on the swap (or rather the loss of any trading profit it would have had without the counterparty's failure).

Where the synthetic asset is a restructured issue, the risk is spread differently. If the bond fails, the investor who holds the synthetic asset loses everything. Although the swap is the direct source of his payment he will get nothing if the cash to meet the other side of the swap is not forthcoming. If the default is temporary or partial, what he gets will depend on the wording of the swap and the swapping bank's reaction to the default. A normal swap allows the non-defaulting party to cancel and claim the cost of replacement from the defaulting party. Once this is done, the swap is over even if the default is cured. If the bond is brought up to date after the swap has been cancelled, the investor will receive payments in the unswapped form. This is certainly better than nothing, but may be a long way from what he wants. It would be possible to write a swap which waived the right of cancellation or handled the risk differently. However this could only reduce the risk to the investor if it increased it for the swapping bank.

If the swap fails, rather than the bond, the investor is left with a bond which pays in a different currency, or at a different interest rate, from the one he needs. The cost will depend on his position, but he should receive the bulk of his expected proceeds, even net of the cost of converting them into appropriate form where that is necessary.

The swapping bank, or other counterparty, has a swap risk on the bond. If the issuer does not pay principal and interest on the bond, the bank loses one side of the swap. The profit or loss on that will depend on the way markets have moved, but the risk is that the bank loses a profit on the broken side, leaving an uncovered loss on the other side of the swap. The swapping bank is not, however, a party to the bond as such. It therefore has no direct or capital exposure to the bond failure.

LOANS BOUGHT AND SOLD

Loan sales, to use the loose phrase common in the market to cover all the various types, create risks for three main parties: the borrowers, the sellers and the buyers. In many cases, however, the total risk is unchanged, or any increase is *de minimis*. Only the incidence of risk between parties changes. There are, under English and American law, three types of legal form a loan sale can take; they roughly coincide with the three types of commercial arrangement.

Subparticipation is the sale of the right to receive interest and principal on a stated loan. In a sense it is merely a form of funding for the seller. The buyer has no direct access to the borrower who may not even know the loan has been sold. Indeed, while English law probably requires the borrower's permission to sell (because of the breach of confidentiality involved in offering it for sale; see below), this permission need only be general; it would be impractical to request it for each sale.

Subparticipation is mostly used for short-term sales. These include loans made by one bank for periods between one day and one year (but mostly less than six months), sometimes for the sole purpose of selling them. They also include the sale of a drawing under a medium-term facility. Bank A may make a five-year commitment to Company B available at a margin over one, three or six months LIBOR. When the company borrows for six months, the bank may turn round and sell the drawing to another bank, who gets a six-month loan, repaid at maturity with interest. He has no obligation to lend further, receives no commitment or other fee, and has no continuing risk beyond the six-month period. The risks in loan sales are least in this type of sale, which is appropriate because the subparticipation probably gives the least protection legally.

A healthy borrower faces little risk on a subparticipation. Because of their short-term nature almost all borrowers whose loans are sold in this way are healthy. (The sale of an unhealthy loan can give rise to claims against the seller if the buyer loses money and can show that the seller knew of, but did not disclose, the weakness.) The risk is mainly that of dealing with an unknown bank. However this only arises when the borrower is in difficulty, and is discussed in more detail below since it applies more seriously to other types of loan sale. Apart from that there is a small risk that the buyer may be a bank from which the borrower might wish to borrow direct; if the buyer has used up all its spare capacity for the particular borrower, and refuses to lend direct as a result, this reduces the borrower's total access to credit. However buyers are usually smaller or regional banks without direct access to strong borrowers. A sensible bank which does buy debt of a valued client will take care to see that it has unused capacity to meet its direct needs.

The seller faces little risk on an individual sale, although some of the operating risks can be cumulatively more important for a bank with an active programme. There is a small risk that the buyer does not pay for the loan, but a careful seller can avoid releasing the asset until payment is in. It is then only bound to pay any interest or principal to the buyer which it has received from the borrower. If the borrower fails to pay, the selling bank has no obligation to pay the buyer; if the borrower pays only part of what it owes, the seller passes on that part only.

The seller runs an operational risk; if it fails to pass on some of the funds it receives it will be liable for interest on the amount when the error comes to light. Since it will have had the use of the money, this is not a great hardship. The more serious operational risk is if it pays to the buyer money which it has not received from the borrower; or if, having sold at a lower rate of interest than the borrower is paying, it forgets to deduct the difference. While the documentation of the sale should certainly allow it to recover, weak documentation might not; or the buying bank might itself be in financial difficulty and be unable to repay. The chances of this happening in any one case must be small; however a bank which runs an active loan sale programme with a wide range of buyers increases the risk of its happening occasionally to a level which justifies establishing sound controls. The same point is true about the risks if a borrower gets into difficulty and restructures, perhaps needing new money. This is most unlikely to happen in any one case, but the risk that it will happen somewhere increases with volume.

The buyer faces the risks involved in lending to the borrower, with some additions. In the first place, the buyer has a risk on the seller. If the seller collapses between receiving funds from the borrower and passing them on, the buyer becomes an unsecured creditor of the seller, with no claim against the borrower which was the basis of its original credit decision. It will recover in bankruptcy whatever percentage other unsecured creditors receive; the bankruptcy of a bank is likely to be a long, slow process. Or the buyer may find that it is dragged into a restructuring of the seller, to avoid bankruptcy. And while restructurings usually aim to recover more than a formal liquidation, they do not always succeed. Finally the buyer faces the risk of lending to a borrower with which it has little or no contact, or resulting ability to monitor or to influence if it sees things going wrong.

All of these risks are more than theoretical. However they are mitigated by the short-term nature of the loans, and by the lack of any obligation on the buyer to re-lend if it has any qualms at all about the borrower's or seller's credit. Although banks need monitoring systems to make sure that they feel these qualms early, the monitoring can be more superficial, as long as it is also more frequent, than with longer-term loans. The main points apply whether the loan sold is a short-term one-off, or a tranche of a longer-term loan. However there is an additional risk in the latter that does not apply to the former. This is similar to the risk discussed above under NIFs, with the selling bank taking the place of the underwriting bank, and raises the same points about the covenants and the seller's wider relationship with the borrower. Buyers of any except the very best names should check the events of default in any agreement of which they buy a tranche. Equally borrowers who allow their loans to be sold need to be aware of this additional risk, and monitor their own ability to keep within whatever events of default they accept.

The second type of sale mechanism is assignment. The exact ways in which this works vary under the laws of different countries, but the general concept is the same. A bank can normally assign only its rights under an agreement, not its obligations. It may assign with the knowledge or approval of the borrower or without. In English law assignment without the borrower's knowledge is an equitable rather than a full legal assignment, with implications that bring the effect closer to a subparticipation. To get the full benefit of a legal assignment in England, the bank needs not only to have the knowledge and consent of the borrower, but also to sell the whole loan, not just part of it.

Assignment is usually used to sell all or part of a medium-term loan to maturity. Because banks can only assign rights, not obligations, the method is most appropriate for a fully drawn loan, preferably in one currency only. In this way the selling bank avoids the risk that the buyer will default, and that the seller will after all have to take a credit risk it thought it had sold. Certainly, to assign a loan that is not fully drawn leaves the seller at risk if the buyer fails at any time when the borrower has any right to borrow new money under the facility.

Where the facility sold is fully drawn, both buyer and seller face the same operational risks as for a subparticipation, but for many payments, instead of one. Depending on the nature of the loan, there may be many interest payments and just one of principal, or several of principal, or even as many of principal as of interest. Whatever the exact details, the number of payments where a mistake can be made is greater, as is the amount of interest involved in relation to a given level of principal. Having said which the same mitigating points also apply.

The buyer is also at risk on the seller for a longer time and more payments than with a subparticipation. However, it should be possible to give notice to the borrower to pay directly to the buyer, where the latter has qualms about the seller's solvency. This is probably inherent where the assignment is with the prior knowledge and consent of the borrower; even here, however, banks should check that there is wording to that effect. Where the assignment is silent, or is advised to the borrower without requiring consent, specific wording is crucial.

Potentially the trickiest additional risks in loan sales arise where the borrower runs into difficulty. The risks relate to all three parties, though in different ways. The borrower runs the risk already touched on under NIFs, of being forced into liquidation or other forms of insolvency earlier than would otherwise happen, or where it would not have happened at all. This may be where the underwriter/seller calls an event of default to avoid lending, on the same pattern as with NIFs, or where the borrower, or its advisers, decides to take the initiative. A company in difficulty may ask for a temporary moratorium on principal, and sometimes interest as well, while it works out a restructuring plan. Sometimes the leading banks work with it to develop the plan, sometimes it calls in an outside adviser to do so and to negotiate the details with the banks. In all cases it asks for concessions to the original agreements, and in all cases it is a condition of the moratorium that all lenders are treated in the same way during it. Usually, too, any plan requires the lenders to accept the pain it inflicts *pro rata* to their expected losses in liquidation.

Even with a small and cohesive group of banks it is hard to reach agreement on such a restructuring. Loan sales, like NIFs, make it more likely that many of the lenders are either banks which thought they were taking a short-term risk or not banks at all. It takes a certain combination of toughness and realism to negotiate a restructuring which can work, combined with knowledge of and faith in the management of the company. Loan sales may make it harder to achieve this combination. Lenders which lack experience in restructuring, or which do not know the company well, may be almost hysterically tough. They may try to tie the borrower up so tightly that management, left with no real ability to manage, cannot honestly accept the scheme. Or they may require a repayment schedule to which no management of integrity can commit itself. Or, sometimes in reaction to the management's refusal to accept the first proposal, they may go too far the other way and leave themselves with no control and management with little incentive to repay debt as fast as possible. One way or the other, there is a greater risk that a rescheduling will either not occur, or will fail to achieve its objectives.

The risk that the seller takes in this situation depends in part on whether it has sold the whole of its loan or has other exposure. Assuming it has remaining exposure, it runs some of the same risks of a failed attempt to restructure as does the borrower, from the other side of that particular fence. It may also suffer from some doubt as to who has what rights and obligations in any restructuring which is proposed or agreed. For instance, suppose Bank A has sold 40 per cent of a particular loan to Bank B. Bank A is close to the company and has other debts outstanding, perhaps in a less favourable state than the sold loan. As a result Bank A is inclined to go along with what it regards as a reasonable proposal, under which its loan is deferred. Bank B, with no relationship, no other loans to protect and little confidence in Bank A's judgement or impartiality does not like this. Must Bank A act against its better judgement to satisfy Bank B? Or if it follows its judgement, will it face a law suit from Bank B? Will Bank B perhaps threaten such a suit in the hope that Bank A will buy back its loan to avoid the suit and keep the restructuring on the path it thinks most likely to succeed?

Suppose further that, instead of selling just one part of the loan, Bank A has sold two or three parts, perhaps 30 per cent each to Banks B, C and D, keeping just 10 per cent for itself. What line does it take if the buyers all have different views and there is no clear majority among them for any solution, or, again, if it strongly dislikes the majority view? Finally, what happens where the proposal requires the lenders to put new money into the borrower? Of course, if the seller and all its buyers agree that this is the correct solution and are willing to provide their share, there is no difficulty. But otherwise?

There is some limited experience on this last point. In two cases within the author's knowledge, the selling bank undertook to meet the new money required in relation to the original loan it had made. It then negotiated separately with the buyer to try to persuade it to take its share, in one case going so far as to ask the agent to talk to the buyer and explain the rationale of the restructuring. However it is not clear that this will provide a precedent for future cases, for three reasons. First, the amounts sold were small and the seller had larger remaining amounts in each case. Secondly, the central bank of the country concerned was involved and applying quite heavy pressure to see that the restructuring did not fail for factional reasons. Thirdly, the borrower was able to offer a market rate of interest and a good prospect of eventual payment in full, which in the event it achieved. The risk for the buyer on these points is to some extent the inverse of that of the borrower and seller. All run the risk of disagreement inhibiting a viable rescue.

There is no doubt that market documentation on these points has still some way to evolve. In particular, some mechanism is needed whereby sellers can split their vote in certain situations, so that the views of the actual lenders can be known. Both borrower and buyer face the risk that the seller will fail and be unable to meet its commitment to lend at the end of the sale period. This may lock the buyer into a medium-term loan or it may force the borrower to repay the loan with funds earmarked for a different use.

The third method of loan sale is known in Anglo-Saxon law as novation, which involves the making of a new loan, on terms identical to the old one, the proceeds of which pay out the old loan. As a result, the parties are in the same position as if the buyer had taken a participation in the original loan and signed the original agreement. Once the novation is complete, there are no risks relating to the sale other than those which would exist if in fact the buyer had been an original signatory.

There are some features which apply to all loan sales which create some risk, often more of inconvenience than loss. These may arise from the change in the bank with which the borrower deals, and the lack of relationship, but can also relate to the buyer's different status. For instance, even when not in difficulty a borrower may need a change in the loan agreement, perhaps to allow it to make an acquisition or increase its rate of investment. This may be harder to obtain from a non-relationship lender – or the borrower may fear it will, which can amount to the same thing. Secondly, there are various clauses in loan agreements, covering withholding tax, or changes in law or other circumstances, which may affect different banks differently. The borrower is naturally anxious that any change in the lending bank, particularly one which it has no ability to reject, should not make these clauses more onerous than they would originally be. Modern documentation on loan sales usually covers this by first giving the selling bank (other than in novation) the right to accept all changes in the agreement without consulting the buyer (unless they extend the maturity, reduce the rate of interest or increase the amount the bank was bound to lend). Depending on the negotiating positions of the parties the agreement may also give the borrower an absolute or qualified right to approve sale of any part of the loan; this is normal with assignment, although often with a 'not to be unreasonably withheld' rider, and inherent in the nature of novation. The position is less clear-cut with subparticipations.

One risk selling banks often take without realizing it is the risk of a breach of confidentiality. Some formal loan agreements contain wording allowing the banks to disclose such information as they consider necessary to potential buyers, thus transferring the confidentiality risk to the borrower. He loses control over what information is disclosed to whom. In most cases this is an acceptable risk; borrowers rarely disclose information to one bank unless they are prepared to allow other banks to see it. Where a borrower must disclose unusually sensitive information to its banks to obtain a loan, then it may need to retain the right to approve any buyer. It probably should insist on the right to veto the release of information to a potential buyer of which it does not approve. Oddly enough the area where a breach of confidentiality is most likely is subparticipation. Where the borrower is a public company, the seller may think it can sell a loan based only on published information and therefore there is no breach in confidentiality. However a bank cannot sell a loan without disclosing its existence, which in other circumstances banks would avoid doing. Even quite experienced lawyers have been known to overlook the point. Some American lawyers think that the practice of loan sales is now so well established in the United States that no permission is needed to breach confidence in this particular way. In mid-1988 English lawyers do not think the same is true in the United Kingdom. However loan sales started later in England than in the United States, so perhaps in due course the practice will become so well established in the British market that no permission will be needed. Banks operating in other countries will still need to check the point, however.

7 Trading Instruments

GLOSSARY

Cap An agreement under which, if a marker rate (such as six-month LIBOR) goes above an agreed strike level, the seller of the cap pays the buyer the difference between the strike rate and the marker rate. This caps the cost of borrowing at the strike rate. Payments relate to a notional principal amount.

Collar A combination of cap and floor. If the marker rate goes above the cap rate, party A pays party B; if it drops below the floor rate, party B pays party A. This confines the effective cost of borrowing/return on investment within a specified range. Party A, an investor, does not wish his return to fall below a minimum level, but is willing to give up the prospect of extra profit from high rates to insure against the low return; Party B, a borrower, cannot risk very high rates, but is willing to give up the benefit of low rates to buy protection.

Floor The reverse arrangement to a cap; the payment now passes if the marker rate drops below the floor rate, thus protecting an investor's return.

Forward rate agreement Two counterparties set a strike rate for a marker such as six-month LIBOR at an agreed date in the future. If the actual rate on that date proves to be higher than the strike rate, counterparty A pays the difference to counterparty B. If the actual rate is lower than the strike rate, A receives the difference. Thus both parties have a set cost or return on an instrument related to the marker and period concerned, again in relation to a notional amount.

FORWARD AND SPOT EXCHANGE

The risks in forward and spot exchange are of two types, credit/trading and settlement. Both parts of the credit/trading risk are greater the longer the life of the contract. A counterparty is more likely to default in five years than in one. And while it is no more certain that a rate will move against the counterparty in five years than in one, it clearly can move further. The risk of loss and its likely size thus both grow with time.

There are some extra questions with trading losses in bankruptcy. Suppose a company fails two years into a three-year contract. Unless there is a formal agreement, as there usually is with swaps but not with forex, the first question is how to define failure. Clearly liquidation is failure in any context, and the law of each country will spell out exactly when the process is deemed to start. But is any form of procedure short of liquidation, such as Chapter 11 in the United States or Administration in the United Kingdom, a default which justifies a counterparty cancelling the contract and claiming damages? Failing a specific definition the answer is not clear. Where such a procedure is merely threatened, the grounds for action are even weaker. And yet if a bank sees a company on the verge of failure, should it not cover the exchange risk which would result from failure on favourable terms, if it can? If the counterparty does fail, it (or at least its other creditors) will benefit, after all, from the lower cost of compensating the bank. On the other hand, if the bank's fears prove groundless, and the counterparty recovers, it will probably hold the bank to the original contract, and the bank now has an open forex position which it did not want and which may be expensive to cover. If the bank is concerned enough about the counterparty's weakness, or if the cost of being caught short is too great, it may still take this risk.

The underlying question is valid with any forex contract but is more important with longer-term ones because the cost of waiting to maturity of the contract is greater. If a bank is in doubt whether a counterparty will meet a contract maturing next week or next month, it is reasonable to wait and see; if met there is no problem, if not there is both a clear-cut event of default and a clear cost of replacing the defaulted contract. To wait a year or more is altogether different, particularly if the bank expects the currency movements to be adverse, thus adding to the cost of default if it docs occur.

It is difficult to define cost or loss. Again, if the contract runs to maturity, it is the extra cost to the bank of buying the currency which the defaulting counterparty should have delivered. But until the contract matures nobody knows for sure what the failure will cost, if anything. On the other hand, it is not sensible to sit and wait while the cost mounts as rates move adversely.

Fortunately the bank can take out a replacement contract, and by doing so establish the cost in a different way. For instance, if Bank A has sold £1 million forward to Company B for $1·8 million and Company B fails a year before the contract matures, Bank A merely has to buy $1·8 million for delivery in one year. If it costs £1·1 million, Bank A can claim the difference of £100 000 between the figure in the original contract and the new cost. Or at least it can unless, when the liquidator comes to examine the now matured claim, he finds that by maturity the rates had moved, so that instead of the replacement costing £100 000 more than the original contract, it would have cost less. He may then argue that Bank A acted wrongly in covering and should have waited until maturity, and refuse the claim. Under Anglo-Saxon laws there is a duty on Bank A to try to reduce the cost of the breach of contract. Most lawyers seem to believe that, provided Bank A can show that covering was a sensible move to mitigate the damages, the courts will uphold the bank's action and claim. However there are no precedents, as far as the author knows; nor is it clear what evidence the bank would have to provide. Would it be enough to show that covering was the accepted way of playing safe, or must the bank produce evidence that it had actual reason to expect rates to move adversely? Nor is the reverse position clear, where the bank does not cover, and later movements in rates suggest that it should have. The size of risk thus cannot be foretold before the failure, and may not be clear even then. Moreover any decision, positive or negative, may add to the loss instead of reducing it.

So far the discussion has covered a single contract. It is more complicated where a bank has many contracts with the same counterparty, at least some of which run in opposite directions, giving some prospect of netting. The risk is first of cherry picking, or a liquidator choosing to continue contracts favourable to him and cancel those which are unfavourable. Netting, which may help to protect against that, can take two forms. First, it may apply when one contract reverses another. A shipowner who had ordered a ship from a Japanese yard, payable in yen, might take out forward cover to protect himself against a stronger yen. After it had strengthened, he might decide that it was unlikely to move further; he could then realize his profit by taking out a contract the other way, for the same amount of yen and the same maturity. Netting the two against each other would leave only a single net payment, from the bank to the client.

In some countries the netting process is automatic and would be upheld in court against a liquidator. In most, however, it requires special measures, and in some it is not even sure that these would be effective. The risk is of taking on a greater volume of transactions than would otherwise be acceptable, and then finding that the liquidator can cherry pick, with the bank having no right to net.

The more complicated form of netting has been introduced to the London interbank market with the approval of the Bank of England and Federal Reserve; it applies both on settlement and in bankruptcy. The bankruptcy part has not been tested in court, and if upheld would reduce the benefit to other creditors of the liquidator adopting profitable contracts and rejecting loss making ones. One can argue that this is unfair to other creditors; or that the present ability to cherry pick is unfair to banks and damaging to the market, of which other creditors are after all a part. The central banks may hope that their support makes it likely that the courts will accept the latter view.

The method nets payments in each currency against each other regardless of the other aspects of the contract. Thus, for instance, if Bank A sells dollars to Bank B against sterling, and then buys dollars from Bank B against Deutschmark, the dollars are netted even though both sterling and DM are paid gross. If there is a third contract for French francs against sterling, the sterling payments will be netted as well, as will any others which involve cross liabilities in a single currency. For settlement purposes the netting will be applied to all payments due between the banks on the same day in each currency. For banks active in the interbank market, there will be major opportunities for netting in this way, both in bankruptcy and on settlement.

The position in bankruptcy may vary from country to country and will carry both legal and documentation risk. The courts may rule that netting is not permitted at all (legal risk); or that it is permitted under stringent conditions which the particular document does not meet in full. Even in the worst case, however, netting should help to reduce settlement risk.

Settlement risk applies in both forms only to spot foreign exchange; with forwards the market risk is already covered by credit/trading risk. With a spot transaction, however, there is the two- or three-day risk between contract and settlement, analogous to that in a securities transaction. The counterparty can fail and leave the bank exposed to a short-term market fluctuation risk. The more important risk is that of paying and not receiving. This relates only to the failure of the counterparty on the day of settlement, or at least its failure to pay on that day followed very soon by the start of its liquidation. The size of the risk therefore depends on how many contracts, for what volume, settle on each day, regardless of the starting date of the contracts, and on how soon the bank can recognize failure so that it does not make settlement payments when the other side stops reciprocating. This calls for a control mechanism geared to the settlement date of contracts, or daily settlement line. Given that the risk relates to the size of monies actually paid, a netting for settlement reduces this risk. The worst that the bank can pay away without return is the net amount, and about half the time it will be a net receiver. It may of course fail to receive the net amount, but this will be smaller, usually much smaller, than the gross amount. Even if the netting is overruled later, the bank will only suffer the trading loss, not the full loss.

In brief, while netting is not yet universally tested as a protection against credit/trading risk in bankruptcy, there is at least a good chance that it will help in some countries. It will not guarantee against any loss at all on settlement risk, but should reduce it in all cases and may eliminate it in some.

INTEREST RATE SWAPS

Interest rate swaps suffer credit/trading risk in broadly the same way as forex contracts, except that the prices which vary to create the risks are the interest rates concerned instead of the exchange rates. A fully matched IRS also carries settlement risk on each payment, but since the payments are in the same currency the risk is more easily controllable. And sometimes the payments are net in any case.

However there are several ways in which interest rate swaps can be mismatched, and these can create some extra risks. The simplest are when the interest payments are not made on exactly the same dates. This can be because the payment dates on a bond fall due on calendar quarters, while the LIBOR dates use slightly more variable month-end adjustments. In this case the risk is still for 100 per cent of the amount paid before receipt of the matching payment. However the risk is short-term, and applies only to one payment which with most swaps will be a small proportion of the total. A similar but greater risk arises where one side is payable annually, the other quarterly or semi-annually. Here the maximum loss is three-quarters of one year's interest.

Sometimes swaps are adjusted in ways which do not affect the ultimate value of the swap itself if all counterparties perform, but may increase the credit risk if they do not. For instance, one side makes a payment at the beginning equal to several years interest, and then pays less than the full market rate for the rest of the period. The discounted value of the payments are the same either way, so that in swap terms there is no significant difference. In credit terms, however, the initial payment is the same as a loan, which each subsequent payment at the below market rate amortizes. The risk of failure now is more than that of a swap; there is an outright loss of the unamortized part of the initial payment as well as any loss on the swap.

A variant of this allows the lower interest payment (or a higher than market payment the other way) in return for a lump sum at maturity. Again the amounts are present valued so that in swap terms the end-result is the same. In this case, however, the credit effect is of a series of loans by the counterparty receiving a less than market rate (or paying an above market one). All of the loans have the same maturity date. If the counterparty defaults in the middle of the swap the full loan contracted for may never be made, but it may default just before the swap matures. In that case the other side is in the same position as a lender, or possibly worse given the lack of precedent for this type of situation in liquidation. The extreme version of this, which creates the maximum credit risk, is the zero swap. The fixed rate payer pays one amount, representing compounded interest, at maturity.

A third situation arises when one counterparty sells its side of the swap. Bank A agrees with Bank B to receive fixed rate interest at 9 per cent per annum in return for floating at six-month LIBOR, on £10 million of notional principal for five years. Two years later, fixed rates for the three years' remaining life of the swap have declined. Bank A therefore sells the right to receive what is now an above market fixed rate to Bank C for a lump sum. Bank C now has a credit risk on Bank B for the amount of that lump sum; again this risk is amortized by the above market rates Bank B pays. However Bank B has no direct obligation for the lump sum which was paid to Bank A.

There are undoubtedly other variations and will be more. However these examples should be enough to highlight the ways in which changes in the form of a swap may add to credit risk even when they make little difference in swap terms.

CURRENCY SWAPS

Currency swaps combine the risks of a forward exchange contract and an interest rate swap. Since they involve an exchange of principal in two currencies, there is the same risk as with a forward exchange contract of failure eliminating a profit from rate movements. There is also settlement risk on the principal payments, which settle in different centres.

Failure before maturity would also mean a risk on the remaining interest payments. The risk would combine interest rate risk, from movements in the respective interest rates, and exchange rate risk on both interest and principal. There is settlement risk on interest payments, and may be mismatch risk of a similar nature to interest rate swaps but with the added currency risk.

Finally both types of swap carry documentation risk. Swaps are most often medium-term, mostly from two to ten years although twenty years or more is possible. Their documentation therefore starts rather like a medium-term loan. It develops differently, first to cover the mechanics of the swap, secondly to adjust to the reciprocal nature of the transaction. For instance, if there is a default, the drafter of the document does not know in advance who will default and needs to use phraseology such as 'non-defaulting party'; there also are possible events such as withholding tax or illegality which may cancel the swap without either party being at fault. A final difference in some cases reflects the reciprocal credit risk; with a loan agreement, the events of default apply only to the borrower, as do ratio covenants, negative pledges, cross default and similar items. With a swap agreement, at least some of them apply both ways.

One documentation risk banks take therefore is of committing themselves to things that only the borrower undertakes in a loan. If they are not willing to do so they may have to forgo the protection of the clause for themselves to avoid giving it to the counterparty. For example, should the cross default cover swaps only or debt as well? Should it apply to affiliates or only to the actual signatory of the agreement? And should it apply to any default or only to defaults above a certain size? If the latter, what size?

From a pure credit point of view banks would like to include debt and affiliates, and make any exclusion as small as possible. This puts them in the driving seat, since they can choose whether to accelerate if a default seems critical. However with a swap the counterparty may refuse to accept these points unilaterally, and stronger banks may even expect weaker banks to accept unilateral points against themselves. (Broadly speaking, the stronger the bank's own credit and the weaker the counterparty's, the better the chance that the bank can get unilateral cross default.) Where the bank is unable to insist on one-way cross default, it must choose between reciprocal cross default or none. Either carries risk. To leave any part of it out increases the risk that the bank will identify a weakening in the counterparty's credit, but be unable to act to reduce the exposure. To agree to it on a reciprocal basis increases the risk that the swap will be cancelled at a bad time for the bank because of a weakness, possibly temporary, in its own business.

As already mentioned, one way of reducing the risk on swaps is netting. Another way is the use of standard master agreements. These in turn allow netting, by making all swaps under them part of the same contract. Thus, bankers and lawyers hope, the liquidator will be unable to cherry pick. The risk is that the standard documentation does not work, either because the courts reject the concepts, or because the drafting is weak.

There are two types of standard master agreement in circulation, while some banks have their own. One master, known as BBAIRS, is put out by the British Bankers Association. All banks operating in London must use this in interbank dealings in interest rate swaps for up to two years, unless the trader specifies otherwise at the time of dealing. BBAIRS allows the interpolation of additional or modifying clauses, but only if they are agreed before the deal is struck. This can be critical because BBAIRS, from a credit point of view, is a bare-bones agreement. Acceptable for the two year interbank deals for which it was designed, it has become widely used in other, less appropriate circumstances; in particular for corporate credits of moderate quality and for periods of more than two years. The risk is that it is used in conditions for which it was not designed, and without the additions necessary to adapt to these conditions.

The ISDA (International Swap Dealers' Association) master has been through two phases. In the first it applied to interest rate swaps in US dollars only; in that incarnation it was not so much an agreement as a series of defined clauses for use in agreements. Despite the name it was designed by American bankers and lawyers for the United States. The second ISDA master can cover interest swaps alone or interest rate and currency swaps together, and has achieved wide though not universal acceptance in New York and London. The concept is excellent, but the drafting is opaque to non-lawyers. (The example quoted in Chapter 4 was taken from this agreement.) The result is that as well as the legal risks (concept unacceptable or drafting does not work) already mentioned, the

ISDA master carries a quite unnecessary risk of costly mistakes because operating clerks do not understand the document.

The final risk on standard master agreements arises from the fact that they are standard. If they turn out to be inadequate in any way, the weakness will affect hundreds of deals for an active bank, maybe thousands in a few cases.

OPTIONS, WARRANTS AND FUTURES

Options are on offer for a variety of products. They have some risks that are inherent to themselves, and some that relate to each product. The risk is different for the buyer and seller of an option. It also differs for a put option and a call option, but in detail rather than in the fundamentals.

The seller of an option takes a small credit risk, but a larger trading risk. The credit risk covers the premium payable up front by the buyer; even this is not much risk because if it is not paid, it is unlikely that the seller will be liable on the option. The trading risk is that the price moves against him by more than the amount of the premium. With a call option this would mean an increase in price. The seller either has to deliver the product at an option price lower than the market price at which he could otherwise sell; or he has to go into the market and buy at the higher market price in order to deliver at the lower option price. With a put option it is the other way round. If the price falls and the buyer exercises the put, the option seller has to pay for the product at the option price, which is then above market.

The buyer of an option takes a credit risk on the seller. The size of the risk depends on the nature of the option and in particular on its maturity. The risk is that the seller fails to deliver, or pay for, the asset when the buyer exercises the option. The buyer then loses the profit it would have made and is unlikely to be able to recover the premium paid. The buyer also takes a trading risk; if the price does not move far enough in the right direction, he will not recover his premium. (Of course in this case the seller's credit will not matter.)

Options are often traded on an exchange, which may guarantee the contract, or the seller may provide margin when the option moves into the money or both. The risk may be a clearing house risk, either on the guarantee or on the control of margin; or a risk that the seller will be unable to provide margin at a time when the price is moving rapidly against it. The buyer (or the exchange) will use the margin to replace the cover provided by the option; the risk of loss is then the amount by which the underlying price can move between the margin becoming due and the new cover becoming effective. This will usually be a matter of a few days only; unless the price of the asset is very volatile the risk should be much less than where there is neither an exchange nor any margin required.

The size of the potential loss will depend on the nature of the asset – specifically the volatility of its price and the maturity of the option. The more volatile the price and the longer the maturity the greater the risk. Where there is margin, the maturity becomes less important; what matters is the short-term volatility. This will decide how far the price can move before the decision to cover is effective.

All options involve settlement risk. Some options are traded, and there will be settlement risk when the option changes hands. There is also settlement risk on both sides when the buyer exercises the option. Whether it is a put or call option, the asset and the option price change hands when the option is exercised. At least that happens when the option buyer actually wants the asset; in other cases there may be a net settlement of the profit. And again where settlement is through an exchange there may be a clearing house risk rather than a settlement risk.

Warrants are similar to call options in that they give a right to buy an asset at a fixed price. They differ in three main respects. In origin, they were issued by companies, usually attached to some other instrument such as a bond, and the asset covered by them was a security, whether debt or equity, issued by the same company. This is still the most common form of warrant, but some warrants are into shares or bonds of a different company or into some precious metal or commodity such as gold or copper. The second main difference is maturity. Options are usually for relatively short periods; warrants can be for five, ten or occasionally more years. Finally, whereas options are issued on a negotiated basis to meet demand, warrants are issued on an underwritten or offer for sale basis as with shares or bonds.

These differences change the emphasis of the risk rather than its underlying nature. For instance, an option to buy a bond of Company X involves both the credit of X and of the option seller. If X's credit deteriorates, the bond will not sell at a high enough price to make the option worth exercising. But if X remains healthy, then the trading risk is of interest rates, and a credit loss requires the option to come into the money and the seller to fail. This second risk is missing in a traditional warrant. With an insolvent issuer there will be no point in exercising the warrant; with a warrant in the money it follows that the issuer is healthy enough to issue a new security for cash.

Where the warrant is into securities of another company, or into bullion or a commodity, the risks are similar to those of an option into the same asset. Indeed it is arguably a misnomer to call these warrants at all; they would be more accurately described as underwritten options. Of course the main reason for issuing warrants into another company's shares is usually that the issuer already holds them; warrants into a commodity are usually issued by a producer or someone who holds the commodity in the normal course of his business. This may reduce the risk of failure to meet the warrants, but is a case by case judgement.

As with options, there is a settlement risk in warrants when trading them during their life, and on exercise. Most warrants are traded on an exchange, sometimes the same one as the underlying asset into which they are exercisable, so that the precise nature of the settlement risk will depend on the exchange's procedures.

Futures are more like a forward agreement than an option or warrant. They are a firm agreement to exchange cash for an asset, or one form of cash for another, at a pre-set price and pre-set date. The main difference between currency futures and a forward exchange contract with a bank is this lack of flexibility. A bank will contract for almost any amount, even if it ends in cents, pence or centimes, and for any odd period. A futures contract is for predetermined round amounts and periods. The futures contracts on the other hand are traded on an exchange or over the counter – which is why they need precise and uniform characteristics. This gives them a liquidity which bank contracts cannot match, despite a limited ability to transfer them.

As well as having similar settlement risks to options and warrants, futures share liquidity risk with them. All three are hedging instruments (or speculative if the buyer chooses to use them that way) and their value depends in part on the ease with which the hedger/speculator can realize or reverse his position without waiting to maturity. The liquidity and therefore the risk attached will depend both on the trading arrangements and depth of market in the option/warrant/future; and in that of the underlying asset. If the latter loses liquidity, it is hard for the hedging instrument to remain liquid.

Finally all three involve taking the risk of the underlying asset. In the case of options and warrants this is at least until the time they decide to exercise and thereafter only if they do so (and with options only on a call rather than a put). Except in the case of the traditional warrant, however, this risk will be independent of the seller of the hedging instrument.

FORWARD RATE AGREEMENTS (FRAs)

The primary risk on an FRA is an interest trading risk. For instance, a six by twelve month sterling FRA, agreed on 15 April 1988 might have a strike rate of 9 per cent. Then on 15 October 1988 the six-month LIBOR might be, say, 10 per cent. The counterparty who needed protection against the rise would receive 1 per cent of the notional face amount from the other; if the rate were 8 per cent instead of 10 per cent, he would pay 1 per cent of the same notional principal. Because he would be paying at the beginning of an interest period instead of at the end as in normal borrowing, the amount actually passing would be discounted to the present value of the amount due.

The trading risk is therefore the extent to which the interest rate for the period chosen can fluctuate in the forward period. For instance, if the notional amount were £1 million, and the rate moved 2 per cent, the profit or loss would be £10 000. However, if instead of a six by twelve month FRA, the deal were six by thirty month, we would then look at the movement in the two year rate. This might move more or less than the six month rate, or might move in the opposite direction. But clearly for a given movement the absolute amount payable would be four times larger than for the six month (before present valuing, perhaps at a different rate).

The size of credit exposure is the notional principal multiplied by the maximum movement in the chosen interest rate for the agreed period. If the view is that the most the six month rate can move in six months is 5 per cent, then for a notional amount of £1 million the calculation is £1 000 000 × 0·05 × 0·5 = £25 000. The calculation for two years, given a maximum expected movement of 5 per cent here too, is £1 000 000 × 0·05 × 2·0 = £100 000. (These both ignore the discounting, since we do not know the discount rate which will apply.) The nature of the risk, as opposed to the size of the exposure, relates more to the first part of the equation. The amount due is actually paid, in the example given, after six months. The credit risk then depends on how likely the counterparty is to fail in that time. A strong counterparty will have only a small risk. Even if the amounts payable run into millions instead of thousands, a sound company is unlikely to fail in that period. Of course if he does there is a credit loss only if rates move so that the defaulter would lose, and the bank profit, by completing the contract. On the other hand, with a two year by three year FRA the risk may be greater in both aspects. The one year rate could change by much more in two years than in three or six months. Equally, there is a greater risk of the counterparty failing in two years than in six months. And while the risk of failure increases over time with any counterparty, it increases faster with a weak counterparty than with a strong one.

CAPS, FLOORS AND COLLARS

The trading risk of these instruments works in a similar way to an option. The buyer of a cap expects to receive a payment if the agreed interest rises above the strike rate, and pays a premium for the privilege. If in fact the rate never exceeds the strike rate, he has lost his premium. If the rate exceeds the strike rate on one or more occasions, he has a profit, or at least a return on his investment in the premium. The size of the return depends on the amount by which the rate exceeds the strike rate, and how often it does so; if the rate is six-month LIBOR, for instance, it will be recalculated every six months throughout the life of the cap. Consistently high rates may mean a payment to the buyer every six months. Low or fluctuating rates may mean small payments, or occasional ones. Whatever the outcome, if the seller fails, the buyer loses the payment(s). He also loses the premium.

The seller has the same risk on the premium as with an option, but with the same proviso that if it is not paid, he probably need not pay under the contract. He has no further credit risk, since the only further obligation on him, to pay outright, is pure trading risk.

Exactly the same principal applies with a floor, except that the focus now is on interest falling rather than rising. With a collar the risk is reciprocal. The agreement may be that A pays B if the rate rises above x per cent, and B pays A if it falls below one-half x per cent, giving B a credit exposure on A if interest rates rise above x, A one on B if they fall below one-half x; neither faces any credit loss if rates stay between the two limits, except loss of cover against future movements which may carry a replacement cost.

HYBRIDS

There are numerous types of hybrid. Debt instruments may carry some sort of equity kicker, perhaps a bond convertible into equity. This normally carries a lower rate of interest than an otherwise similar straight bond. The lower rate may marginally improve the credit, but it also reduces the return to the investor by more than this benefit. The return increases only if the price of the equity rises to a level where the conversion is profitable. If this never happens, the convertible bondholder ends up with the same credit risk as the straight bondholder, but less return to compensate for it.

Broadly the same is true where bonds are sold with warrants into equities attached, except that the warrants may carry a price which reflects the value of the equity, rather than this being taken out of the coupon on the bond. Nevertheless the end-result is similar. A company can issue a convertible at par, but at a yield below the market for the straight debt; or it can issue a bond at par, with a market yield but with a warrant attached the price of which reduces the effective cost of the bond. The only difference is that the warrant holder may sell the warrant and realize some of the equity interest before the share price rises, while keeping the bond, whereas the convertible holder can realize value in the equity kicker only by selling, or converting, the whole.

The requirements of the regulators have introduced a special version of the convertible for banks. This is a subordinated loan, bond or preference share which converts into equity only if some disaster occurs. This is most likely to be an inability of the issuing bank to pay a dividend. The bank wishes to count the debt as part of its capital for regulatory purposes. The regulators will agree to this only if the debt can be used to absorb losses and thus protect the depositors and other senior creditors; they achieve this by the enforced conversion. The result is that the holder accepts an equity risk without getting any assurance of an equity return. Unlike a normal convertible, these carry a higher than usual rate to compensate for the risk, but it is still a fixed rate with no share in profits. Admittedly, if the holder is forced to convert, the issuing bank may recover and the equity regain value to a level where the holder ends up making an equity profit. But the holder has no control over whether to convert; and is forced to convert at just the time when an unrestricted investor would be least likely to do so. So, while a happy ending is theoretically possible, it is not expected.

There are also hybrids which go to make up some of the individual products. For instance, when a bank lends foreign currency, it may simply take a deposit in that currency; or it may go out and take a deposit in a different currency and swap it into the currency lent. The borrower neither knows nor cares in most cases. He has the funds he wants in the currency he wants at the interest rate he wants. The bank therefore faces a normal lending risk on him; but on the other side instead of having a deposit alone it has a deposit and a swap, with a credit risk on the swap counterparty which would not exist with a simple deposit.

Similarly, with a collar, a bank may match it against offsetting transactions with other counterparties. In some cases, however, it will achieve the same, or even a better, trading result by some highly sophisticated use of options and swaps. Here again there may be an additional, or merely different, credit risk as a result. If the bank recognizes the credit risk and is satisfied that the trading benefit outweighs it, no harm is done. The concern remains that the bank either fails to recognize the risk altogether, underestimates it, or fails to take simple protective action that would reduce it.

There are too many varieties of hybrid to permit discussion of them at length. The point is that they are often seen as merely trading risks because they are constructed by the trading desk to match a product where the bank has recognized and approved the credit risk. Banks have systems which require separate credit approval for any transaction which involves a credit risk. These systems will only work, however, if the traders recognize that there is a credit risk to be approved.

Part IV

Risk/Reward

8 Capital Adequacy

GLOSSARY

Basle Committee/Cooke Committee/G10 The group of central bankers, chaired by Peter Cooke of the Bank of England, who designed the capital adequacy requirements proposed for commercial banks of all countries in the group.

Capital adequacy (ratio) The regulatory and prudential concept that banks need a minimum level of capital to ensure them against being bankrupted by normal loss. The level depends on the nature of their assets and the risks attributed to them, and is best expressed as a ratio or percentage of capital to assets.

Loan equivalent The amount that a bank or counterparty could actually expect to have at risk in a failed company, rather than the face amount of the transaction.

Mark to market The practice of valuing trading assets or positions in line with current market levels. The practice shows the profit or loss in a position, or its balance sheet value; and thus, when needed, the exposure to loss in a position the value of which depends on a counterparty's credit standing.

INTRODUCTION

The first seven chapters of this book have focused on risk, on the grounds that unless banks and bankers understand the nature of risk, they cannot judge when to accept and when to reject it; or when to insist on a higher return or more protection. The book recognizes that some risks are small; some are easy for banks to protect themselves against; some provide a large reward; and above all banks are in business to take risks and to be paid for taking them. Successful banks recognize which risk falls into which category, protect themselves at a cost which leaves a reasonable profit overall, accept the small risks without fuss provided that there is some reward, and ensure that when they take the greater risks the reward is commensurate.

To do all of this banks need to understand the nature of each risk not just absolutely, but compared to risk on alternative products.

They also need to understand the costs of each transaction. It is easy to forget that some transactions are more complicated and expensive to operate than others; some require more (expensive) capital cover than others; and some have a different relationship between exposure and risk than others. A return on exposure which implies a fair return on risk in one case may be either wholly inadequate or very generous in others.

In brief, while some risks may seem hardly worth bothering about, this is not true. Even small risks can turn nasty if neglected; and all unnecessary losses are expensive. Banks are in business to take risks, but they will only succeed if they recognize the corollary. Successful risk taking means recognizing, controlling, minimizing and being paid appropriately for risk. Failure to recognize risk, or cost, virtually guarantees failure; recognition does not guarantee success, but makes it more likely.

CAPITAL REQUIREMENTS FOR DIFFERENT RISKS

Because banks take a wide spread of risks, it is inevitable that some will go wrong. It is not inevitable that the losses will be large or concentrated in any one year so that the bank loses more than its annual profit on other business, but it is possible. To guard against this a bank needs capital. The amount depends on a range of factors, not all of which are relevant to this book. For a commercial bank, a key factor is the nature and quality of the credit risks it takes. This includes the overall make-up of the portfolio – concentration on one or a few types of borrower; number of large individual exposures; average life of loans, level of amortization/liquidity; geographical spread; breakdown between loans to government, banks and corporates and what sort of corporates; wholesale or retail; and a range of other factors.

Within the portfolio, too, the requirement depends on the type of instrument giving rise to the risk, and on the quality of the bank's credit controls and thus of the credit risks it is taking.

The risk of a loan, in this sense, is straightforward. If a borrower goes into liquidation owing the bank $10 million, that is the amount the bank can lose, the amount by which its capital can reduce, and the risk against which it needs to keep capital. Since the loan is only one of many, few of which will fail, the bank need cover only an amount which conservatively reflects the chances of loss in the whole portfolio.

With other products, settlement risk for instance, either the exposure or the risk may be less. If the settlement is guaranteed DVP, the exposure is only the market movement risk, while where settlement is non-DVP, it is 100 per cent plus the market risk. However, while it is possible to lose the whole amount, the risk is reduced by the short time involved and the self liquidating nature of the underlying transaction. Settlement risk thus requires some capital cover, but less than for a loan.

Because they do not appear on the balance sheet, and sometimes not even in footnotes, off balance sheet items were not caught by capital adequacy ratios previously imposed by some central banks. For this reason, among others, banks tended to keep lower levels of capital against these risks than against comparable on balance sheet risks. In some cases they steered business into forms which were off balance sheet and priced them as if they needed no capital. The rates banks quote to underwrite NIFs and so on is only the most obvious example of this. This, combined with bad debts due to poor lending practices, helped to make many banks undercapitalized. It also led to tighter regulation by central banks and may even have played a part in getting the G10 rules accepted.

The idea that off balance sheet risks are *ipso facto* less than on balance sheet, and that they need less capital, does not bear analysis. A commitment to lend, for instance, carries the same exposure whether the loan is outstanding today or not. If it is, the worst that can happen is that the company fails and repays nothing; if it is not, the worst that can happen is that the company draws it down, fails and still repays nothing. The loss in either case is identical.

Some bankers argue that the risk is less where the commitment is not being used. Sometimes the bank can cancel it before it is used, or the company may fail before using it. A few commitments are available for purposes which the borrower cannot meet because of its weakness; a few others give the bank the right to cancel before the company draws if it is alert enough to exercise it.

A prudent bank will recognize that these mitigations do not happen often and are largely out of its control; a sinking borrower is more likely to draw the facility fully in a desperate effort to save itself. Banks should therefore treat the risk and capital requirement of an undrawn commitment in much the same way as a loan made under the same commitment. Perhaps in looking at sizeable portfolios they might make some allowance for non-usage, and take overall commitments as requiring, say, 80 per cent or 90 per cent capital cover, but no less.

Apart from anything else, a bank with low capital cover on its commitments may find itself in a nasty position if the percentage usage rises rapidly. Commitments taken on in easy money conditions may only see 25–35 per cent usage as long as easy money lasts; backstops for NIFs and the like will see less. If money becomes tight, usage of traditional commitments may rise to 50–60 per cent, sometimes more. We have no experience of usage of NIF backstops in tight money, but an increase from perhaps 5 per cent to 50 per cent does not seem excessive; nobody can say that even 80–90 per cent is impossible. A level of capital barely enough to cover the lower usage with small allowance for the unused will see a bank with large commitments in serious difficulties if usage rises suddenly.

It is harder to allocate a reliable capital cost to some other products. Swaps are an example. Some banks calculate the exposure at the beginning, based on assumptions about the likely movements in interest or exchange rates during the life of the swap. Others, and the G10 regulators, mark the swap to market regularly and then add something for risk of further fluctuations during its remaining life. This means that for regulatory purposes the capital required for a swap will vary, possibly quite sharply, throughout its life. This makes it hard to know what allowance for capital the bank should make in its pricing (which must be decided at the time of dealing); and in controlling its level of capital cover to ensure that it always has enough even when risks turn sour on a larger than expected scale.

The G10 capital adequacy requirements, discussed further in a later section, should force banks to look at ways to handle this problem, not just as it relates to swaps but to all the major existing products, and to new ones as they develop.

LOAN EQUIVALENTS

One approach is to develop a method of converting the risk in each product into an amount at risk comparable to that of a loan. Some banks call this loan equivalents, others risk equivalents and no doubt there are other names. But the idea is simply to demonstrate the amount that can be lost, on worst reasonable assumptions, and equate these to the amount that can be lost on a loan.

Two examples may illustrate the first approach. First, the market element of settlement risk in a guaranteed DVP situation. The risk here is the amount that the price can move in the period between agreeing the sale and settling it, plus an allowance for delays in covering. Take a hypothetical example. Bank A agrees to buy from Bank B $1 million worth of Ruritanian government bonds at face value on the Ruritanian exchange. Under Ruritanian rules, settlement is due two days later, guaranteed DVP by the Ruritanian Central Bank. On the due date Bank A pays its $1 million to the Central Bank, but the following day the Central Bank returns the money with a day's interest and advises that Bank B is unable to deliver and has gone into liquidation. The amount Bank A actually loses will depend on how far, if at all, the price of the bond has risen; it may actually have fallen and Bank A made a profit by buying it cheaper. The amount it *could* lose (the exposure) depends on how long it takes to buy the replacement bond and the volatility of the bond's price. In an active and liquid market it should be easy to cover by the third day and the largest remotely likely price rise in that period might be three per cent. Three per cent, or $30 000 in the example, might then be the loan equivalent; or we might be a little more conservative and say that the failure of a bank risks upsetting the market and delaying the ability to buy in, and we might use 5 per cent or $50 000. And of course if the instrument being bought were a junk bond, with a volatile and illiquid market; or if the settlement period were five, seven or even twenty days, we might need a loan equivalent of 10–25 per cent. Whatever the figure, it will be less than the $1 million transaction from which it derives.

The loan equivalents of different settlement risks can thus vary quite widely. In each case it depends on a combination of the speed of the settlement system and the volatility of the instrument. Even a fairly stable instrument can change price substantially if the settlement takes weeks rather than days. And of course where settlement is not guaranteed DVP the 100 per cent risk of paying and not receiving is added to the percentage market movement risk.

In the second example Bank A agrees to pay Bank B 4 per cent fixed in Swiss francs for five years in return for six-month LIBOR, which at the time is 3½ per cent. Bank A may expect six-month LIBOR to rise sharply or may have a swap the other way at better rates and want to lock in a profit. It is at risk if Bank B fails when six-month LIBOR is above 4 per cent. But at the time the swap is done nobody knows any of the critical information needed to calculate what Bank A's claim would be – whether Bank B will fail, if so when and what rates will be at the time. Therefore a loan equivalent can only be what the lawyers call a 'genuine pre-estimate of damages'. There are broadly speaking two ways of doing this at the time the swap is agreed.

One is to use a fixed percentage for each year of the swap's life. This may be the same for all swaps or may vary with currency or other details, but be standard for all swaps within a certain type. For instance, a bank might use 2 per cent of face value for each year of a sterling interest rate swap. A three-year swap would then have a loan equivalent of 6 per cent of the notional principal of the swap, a five-year swap of 10 per cent and so on.

Another approach, which can have many variations of detail, is more complex. It starts by making certain assumptions about the movement of interest rates, using the fixed rate in the actual swap as a base. It might, for instance, assume that interest rates doubled or halved, depending which side the bank was taking, over, say, the next three years, and thereafter remained unchanged. The bank can then calculate the cost of replacing the swap if the counterparty fails at any given point, and thus also the cost if the counterparty fails at the worst possible moment; or it can use the average cost given that failure is equally likely at any time in the life of the swap. With a cross-currency swap the approach is modified to take account of the volatility of the exchange rates but is similar in principal. Different assumptions about interest rates and currency volatility can be used for different currencies, but since the underlying assumption is based on the starting rate it will tend to adjust to different market conditions better than a flat percentage. To use the results of these calculations effectively probably means each banker who has to make credit decisions on swaps should have a floppy disc or programme on a personal computer, into which to feed details of the swap. (The regulators' approach of mark to market plus future exposure amounts to the same thing when taking the decision. At that time the mark to market is by definition nil, since the swap is being done on the market; the whole exposure is therefore future exposure. All that can vary is the method of calculating it.)

The little experience there is of credit losses on swaps suggests that, at least in dollars, the worst possible moment calculated as suggested above is reasonably accurate. However only as we see a range of losses wide enough to provide a sound statistical base will we know whether this is indeed the case or just a freak result.

Then there is the question of whether a bank should reduce the level of capital as a swap approaches final maturity. Logically as each interest payment is made the risk of loss should be less. However if interest rates move sharply the immediate effect may be to increase the cost of replacing even the smaller number of payments. On the other hand the notional cost on a given assumption about future interest rates will be lower after each payment than before, as will an allocation of risk at 2 per cent per annum. The combination of mark to market and future exposure may provide the answer. Mark to market shows what the loss would have been had the counterparty failed yesterday, or if it failed before the next payment with no change in rates. The two together may give a clue as to whether the combination of rate movements and the passage of time has increased or reduced the remaining exposure. This is presumably why the Cooke Committee chose to use the combination for capital adequacy calculations.

Even when we have a loan equivalent exposure, this may not be enough; it measures the worst that can happen, but not the risk that it will happen, and this is arguably as important. It is true that a ten-year loan for $10 million, and a settlement risk on a $10 million bond purchase, without guaranteed DVP, can both in theory lose a bank $10 million. But a bank which has both risks to the same, wide, range of clients will lose more on the ten-year loans than on the settlement risk. It therefore needs more capital to guard against loss on the ten-year loans.

This leads on to the concept of risk adjusted loan equivalent (RALE), which takes a particular type of loan, probably a one-year loan, as the basis and adjusts all other loan equivalents to it. Thus, for example, if the view is that a bond settlement's loan equivalent involves 5 per cent of the risk of a one-year loan, but a ten-year loan involves twice the risk, we can say that:

(a)	$10 million of bond settlement risk	= RALE $500 000 plus;
(b)	$10 million one-year loan	= RALE $10 000 000 plus;
(c)	$10 million ten-year loan	= RALE $20 000 000;
(d)	Total therefore	= RALE $30 500 000.

This approach is undoubtedly useful in looking at the portfolio as a whole, and can be even more so with one further adjustment to allow for the quality of the borrower/counterparty. Thus the RALE benchmark might apply to a one-year loan to a corporate borrower rated BBB; a similar loan to a borrower rated AAA might be only RALE 85 per cent. A ten-year loan to an AAA borrower might be RALE 140 per cent against the RALE 200 per cent for a ten-year loan to a BBB rated borrower. (These percentages are hypothetical and illustrative only; to use the system in reality would require much statistical and other analysis to demonstrate the true relationships. Even then ratings are to a degree subjective; if the approach to ratings changed, or if an approach developed for the US market were applied to European markets for which it was not intended, the results could be misleading. On the other hand, provided the errors are not too large, it may be helpful to compare apple with apple even though we do not know what brands they are. The present system is more like trying to compare apples with what we think are pears, but may really be bananas and oranges.)

Applied with proper care, the idea of RALE has some real benefits in assessing a portfolio. Its value is more suspect in applying it to individual names and decisions. A portfolio of AAA-rated names should not change vastly over time, or even its strength relative to a similar sized portfolio of BBB-rated names. A tendency to overrate some names will balance a tendency to underrate others. The average may be about right, but not every single name that makes up the sample.

Then again, RALE mixes the concepts of risk and exposure. This does not matter when looking at a portfolio. The same exposure on term loans and settlement risk can carry a different likelihood of loss, as demonstrated earlier. Over a large enough portfolio the amount actually lost will reflect this difference, but this does not apply to individual names. Thus, if loan equivalent settlement exposure on a particular instrument is $1 million, and the counterparty fails, the bank has the whole $1 million at risk. Even though the chance of failure is only 5 per cent of that on a one-year loan, the amount that can be lost is the same. A system which showed the RALE as $50 000 could lead an inexperienced banker, or even an experienced banker deciding in a hurry without paying full attention, to approve a $50 000 RALE thinking that the exposure was $50 000. The subsequent actual loss of $1 million could be wholly out of proportion to the reward the bank was getting.

RALE also underestimates the impact of repetitive transactions. Consider two reasons why a settlement risk is less than a one-year loan of the same amount. First, there will only be an actual loss if the counterparty fails on, or very shortly before, the day of settlement; it must fail, or the bank must learn of its failure, after the bank has irretrievably committed itself to payment, but before the counterparty has made the offsetting delivery. The chances of that happening where the bank settles with a counterparty only once, or even once every month or so, is clearly less than the chance that the borrower of a one-year loan fails at some time during the year. Where the bank settles with the counterparty virtually every day, the risks are closer to each other. It is easy to forget that the risk changes when we move from a single transaction to a line for continuous usage.

The second argument for the lower risk on even a continuously used settlement line is that the bank can easily stop dealing. It will then be a matter of days only before the outstanding transactions are cleared and the bank has no further risk. In other words the quality of monitoring needed, and the level of foresight, to avoid loss is much less. The chance of being caught by a rapid deterioration and finding the party bankrupt while the bank is exposed thus depends heavily on the speed with which the bank can withdraw.

There are two snags to this argument. One is the risk of complacency. The knowledge that it can get out quickly may make the bank less inclined to monitor carefully, which then reduces the chance that it will see trouble coming in time to duck. In other words a long lead-time plus careful monitoring need not be much riskier than a short lead-time with poor monitoring.

Secondly, it does not follow that a bank can always get out of a facility quickly, just because the transactions covered are short-term. If the continuance of the facility is essential to the client's ability to stay in business, it may not be easy to withdraw until the client has found another bank to provide the service. If the bank is providing a unique service, or is one of a few banks providing it, there may be a utility element which inhibits withdrawal even when it might otherwise seem fully justified. (Euroclear, Cedel and the few banks providing American Depository Receipt (ADR) services all face this problem to a greater or lesser degree.) Of course, in an extreme case, a bank might overrule these considerations; however, if by doing so it bankrupts the company it runs three risks. First and least likely (but possible anywhere and more likely in some countries than in others) it risks lender's liability; if the company or its creditors can argue that the bank's action caused the bankruptcy unnecessarily, the cost may be much greater than the loss caused by staying in the picture. Secondly, even if this is avoided, the risk that the bank will in fact cause bankruptcy before it is paid in full, or so soon after it that the bankruptcy courts recall the payment, is a real one. Thirdly, if it has other exposure to the counterparty, its action to protect short-term exposure may increase the risk on long-term exposure.

In brief, the arguments in favour of loan equivalents are strong; only the difficulty of calculating them and agreeing them holds back what must be a certain move in their direction. RALE, while attractive in some ways, is less certainly desirable.

RETURN ON CAPITAL, ON ASSETS AND ON RISK

A bank, like any other company, needs to earn a return on its capital. The return can come from high leverage (that is, many assets in relation to capital) and a low return on assets, or from lower leverage and a higher return on assets. Equally the risk related to the assets can be high so as to earn a high return, or both can be lower. Or the bank can earn a higher return on assets by providing a high quality service which enables it to charge more than other banks, or by putting emphasis on products and services which generate revenue directly through fees rather than through assets, and thus use less capital. Such services usually either need a high degree of skill, which is expensive in itself and may carry high overheads, or they involve high risks of a non-credit nature. If these risks go wrong the return disappears, along with some of the capital.

There is a tension between these various requirements whose resolution calls for skilled management. The intensive competition in international banking in the 1970s and 1980s aggravated this tension; the growing tendency for investment banks to compete in what had previously been commercial banking markets; the rapid development of new 'investment banking' products to meet needs previously met by commercial banking products; the emphasis on marketing these products quickly while they were still 'proprietary'; the tendency to overlook risk in the rush to get business; and the resulting downgrading of risk specialists, and perhaps especially credit specialists, at a time when arguably the need for their knowledge was greater than ever; all of these contributed to the general weakness in many banks and banking systems by the late 1980s. The emphasis of many banks on size rather than profits, at least until the mid-1980s, also contributed.

In particular they made the conflict between return on equity (ROE), return on assets (ROA) and return on risk (ROR) harder to solve. Competition for assets meant that the ROA generally declined, so that to maintain their ROE banks needed either more assets on the same capital base (higher leverage) or higher yielding assets. The growing demand for assets, particularly high-yielding assets, tended to reduce the yield on all assets, and to squeeze the differential between return on levels of risk. The lower ROA and ROE added to the vicious spiral by pushing up the leverage needed for a given ROE still further. In time leverage, and a perceived decline in the quality of many banks' assets, began to affect the cost of funds and of capital, thus making it even harder to earn adequate returns.

At the same time the best corporate credits began to raise funds from the new capital market products, leaving the commercial banks to lend to lower quality names, but with steadily decreasing returns to offset the lower quality. As the discrimination between levels of bankable credit was eroded, banks earned lower returns for higher risk than ever before. When this came home to roost, as it did in specific cases such as Continental Illinois and Penn Square, and in more general cases such as Latin American debt, the viability of major banks and whole banking systems was threatened. And yet, even in mid-1988, there were only tentative signs of banks being able to increase margins on lending or other credit products; they still need to improve the return on capital and the balance between risk and return.

The move to off balance sheet assets was in part due to this. Too many banks, however much they now deny it, saw unused NIF stand-bys and similar instruments as something which did not affect reported leverage. On this view, the earnings were free of any higher need for capital and thus, however small, improved the return on equity.

Outside commentators, central banks, the rating agencies and securities analysts have been gradually becoming aware of the danger of this sloppy thinking. The Bank of England was probably the first regulator to take formal action, but it was the combined effort of the Bank and the Federal Reserve which first produced a reasoned code for the treatment of off balance sheet items, a code since adopted with modifications by G10.

The G10 capital adequacy requirements, perhaps aided by the downgrading of a number of banks by Moodys and Standard & Poors, may help to solve the problem. The many banks which are short of the G10 requirements have broadly four ways of meeting them. They can raise new capital in the markets, which will require a return, especially for those that are short of equity rather than second-tier capital. They can sell assets; if they sell profitable assets at above book value this may increase capital as well as reducing assets, thus improving both sides of the equation. The sale may however reduce profits, partly offsetting the benefits; or the opposite may be true, with sale of a loss-making asset at below book value reducing net worth more than *pro rata* to assets, but improving earnings. Thirdly the bank can be more selective in its criteria for taking on new assets, aiming only for those which give a high return on the capital they use. For many banks this will cause a decline in assets, and for some a slower growth. Desirable in themselves, these two results may mean a gradual improvement in margins generally; the less banks are prepared to throw money at products at ludicrous prices, the better the likely profit margin for those who continue to provide them.

An alternative way of reducing assets, and the fourth way of improving capital adequacy, is to lower the acceptable level of risk. This may mean a lower immediate return on assets, but it also means less assets and less need for capital. Moreover, unless the bank's pricing and credit controls were excellent, there is a prospect that the assets were not paying enough in relation to the risk; in this case the longer-term return on assets may improve. This approach too may have the advantage of reintroducing some credit discrimination into pricing. If enough banks reduce the volume of assets they will take, raise the return at which they will take them or reduce the risk attached to them, there should be a general improvement in margins, and a greater one on higher risk assets.

That said, there is a good deal of scepticism among banks as to whether these desirable trends are likely. None of the logic behind the arguments is new, although G10 gives some of them more muscle. If banks have ignored them so far, despite the damage this has done, why should they suddenly change? And even if they do change, will they change enough, and indeed how far is enough?

As far as the author knows, there has been no comprehensive study of what return on equity, assets or risk the G10 requirements imply. What follows certainly does not claim that description, but may indicate some of the questions that need answering. However, it focuses only on the G10 requirements, which largely ignore non-credit risks. Given that some products earn high returns with little credit risk but need capital to cover other risks, it may be wrong to calculate returns without further adjustment. Nevertheless, the discussion may show the size of the adjustment needed to allow banks to continue to charge current low returns for credit.

First, what is meant by capital? For this discussion, we assume that the G10 definitions for first-tier capital exactly match the market's concept of the equity on which it calculates return; and that the average cost to banks of second-tier capital is 2 per cent above the normal cost of funding which the bank meets before calculating return on capital. We assume, too, that the strong banks have a lower minimum imposed on them by their central banks, say 5 per cent first-tier and 5 per cent second-tier, while the weaker banks have, say, 6 per cent and 6 per cent.

The second question is what level of return on capital banks need. For a bank which is short of the G10 requirements, the right figure may be the cost of capital in the market; this may be higher than its existing cost of capital because it is having to raise it in large amounts from a position of weakness in an unfavourable market. A bank which already has more capital than the G10 requirements may be more inclined to look at its return on capital; it will want to be sure it can earn the same return on any new capital required as on the existing capital. One way of ensuring this is to insist on a return now which allows it to increase capital from retained earnings rather than going to the market.

The question of whether a bank looks at cost of capital or desired return on capital has one odd effect. Stronger banks are likely to have a higher return on capital but a lower cost than weaker banks. We could see a situation where strong banks require a higher return than weak banks; if they are able to command it, the gap between strong and weak will steadily widen.

For the discussion, however, we will assume that both banks use a desired return, but that the strong bank wants 20 per cent on equity, while the weaker will accept 12 per cent. We will also apply the criteria initially to a $10 million fully drawn loan to a corporate borrower rated AAA. What follows also ignores direct earnings on the capital, and the fact that ROE is after tax, while the returns discussed are pre-tax; we assume that they offset each other. Any bank trying to work out the true impact of the G10 requirements would need detailed analysis of many of these points. See Table 8·1.

These margins, which should be further increased to allow for operating costs and the risk of default to any less than AAA borrowers, are so far above those ruling in mid-1988 as to make it unlikely that banks will obtain them. The reservations about whether Basle is right to concentrate only on credit risk may also have some impact here. Short-term rates for AAA names are often below LIBOR, and bank loans for five years or more rarely above LIBOR +25bp in the early years.

Table 8.1

	Strong bank	*Weak bank*
1st tier	$500 000	$600 000
Return needed	@ 20% = $100 000	@ 12% = $72 000
2nd tier	$500 000 @ 2% = $10 000	$600 000 @ 2% = $12 000
Total return needed	110 basis points	84 bp
Funding cost	LIBOR−35	LIBOR−10*
Margin over LIBOR	75bp	74bp

*This is generous. A really weak bank might fund at LIBOR flat or even LIBOR +.

Commitment fees fall into a similar category; on the one hand, despite what was said above about relative risk, most regulators including G10 allow a lower capital requirement, 50 per cent, or less depending on the maturity and type of commitment. Still, 50 per cent would leave a requirement of 55 or 42 basis points on the assumptions set out above, since there is no opportunity to make funding profits, and there is nothing in the figure for operating or default costs. This compared, in mid-1988, with commitment or facility fees for NIFs and the like often below 10 basis points. Even where there are front-end fees or fees for utilization, they do not add much to the return on a longer-term facility.

For many products there are front-end fees, and for all types of facility there are various degrees of hope or certainty of other profitable business, so that it does not follow that all banks are losing money lending at present rates. Where some of the other business only seems profitable because it is off balance sheet, but is about to be brought on balance sheet, its price may have to rise or its value as compensating business fall. Indeed some off balance sheet instruments may become unprofitable when they have to meet a full capital allocation, unless their return rises. This in turn may help some of the conventional products raise their return without becoming wholly uncompetitive. This will only really work, however, with a generally agreed set of loan equivalents. All parties – banks, regulators and clients – must be able to see how the capital cost and risk of various items relate to each other.

All banks need not take exactly the same view of all loan equivalents. There is always room for judgement as to the exact level of risk; and in many cases the bank itself can increase or reduce the risk by the way in which it handles it. Legitimate differences of professional opinion are essential to the sound working of the market; however, the market will not work well if banks reach opinions in a vacuum, or if their judgements start from such different bases that they are not really judging the same thing.

PRUDENTIAL REGULATION – A BLESSING OR A CURSE?

There is an argument that banks know their business better than any regulator can; and that in any case they are subject to the pressures of the market. This argument would do without prudential regulation altogether, or at least keep it to a minimum. A slightly different version suggests that the regulators should compel the weaker banks only to do what the best banks are already doing, not load them all down with bureaucratic requirements that hurt everybody.

The stronger argument is that banks need prudential regulation for three main reasons. First, they carry so much of the economy in their deposits that to allow them to collapse has a far wider-reaching impact than the failure of almost any other type of company. Secondly, competition between banks is now international; in many countries the market is either imperfect, opaque or simply not relevant. It is hard to say, for instance, that an American or British bank, quoted on the stock exchange and relatively open in its accounting, is on the same footing as a nationalized European bank, whose remit from its owner may have little to do with profits or with prudent banking; or as a Japanese bank which is subject to inscrutable directives from the Ministry of Finance, but also to its support in times of trouble. Or as both Japanese and European banks whose true strength we are not allowed to know because of hidden reserves. These may be massive and make the banks better capitalized than their Anglo-Saxon brethren. Even if this is true, which some sceptical Anglo-Saxons doubt, how will we know when imprudent lending or other losses start to eat into these reserves? Because we never know what they are, we shall not know when they are gone. While this point is often expressed in terms of level playing-fields, it is deeper than that. Whatever the ability of an unfettered market to impose prudent practices on banks, the fact is that the market is heavily fettered at the moment.

The third reason is that under the present mixed regime banks as a whole and many banks individually are managing themselves poorly. If a magic wand were to present all banks with equal opportunity, and leave them subject only to the discipline of a suddenly perfect market, the result would be turmoil. It would damage so many economic and political interests that somebody would very quickly 'unwave' the wand. Indeed, while there is no reason to suspect that G10 is a move towards prudential deregulation in banking, something like it would probably be a necessary first step. Only when banks were generally properly capitalized, strongly managed and more transparent in their accounting than they are now, could even the most ardent proponent believe that free markets alone would exercise enough discipline.

Against this background, added to an exploding market in bank products, losses in Latin America and elsewhere, and a general decline in the strength of commercial banks, regulators began to address the fact that their old methods were no longer working well; at a time, moreover, when deregulation in other areas made prudential regulation more necessary. It also made it vital that regulators co-operate to develop a form of regulation which would work internationally. The level playing-field argument has been made strongly by its advocates, but there are other important points involved.

The Bank of England and the Federal Reserve took the first step in proposing a joint set of regulations to cover banks of both countries. This proposal was then taken up by the Cooke Committee, representing regulators of the Group of Ten countries, meeting in Basle, and agreed by them with some modifications. The G10 proposals allow central banks some flexibility on certain points and cater for differences in national practices, but the overall aim is to have a similar set of regulations applying to all banks. This should mean that no bank has an advantage over its competition simply because one central bank is a slacker regulator than another. More importantly, it means that all creditors of a bank, whether clients, investors in debt or equity of the bank, or other banks dealing with it in a variety of markets, will have a clearer idea of its credit standing. There is of course no guarantee against failure; there is, or should be, a reduced risk of failure and an improved ability to see warning signs in advance. If this last point proves correct, then the market may begin to exercise some prudential pressure on banks, supplementing the regulators' efforts.

It also means that all banks, not just those more or less exposed to market pressures, should have a clear and similar incentive to operate soundly. In the medium to longer run this will strengthen the credit standing of the banking system. It should also improve its risk assessment techniques, especially but not solely credit risk. This in turn should make banks better allocators of resources to priority users, which is after all one of their key economic functions.

This is not the place to discuss the details of G10. The key points, however, are relevant to the theme of this book. The effect of G10 can be summarized under several headings:

(a) It insists on the need for a minimum level of capital against credit risk, with upward variations where a bank is in businesses which involve higher risk in other areas, or has suspect controls.
(b) It defines two levels of capital – first- and second-tier, which might be called pure equity and effective capital, and the relationship they must bear to each other within the minimum total.
(c) It clarifies the need to keep different levels of capital against different risks; and goes some way towards defining the levels of risk and how to assess them. (It is perhaps in this area that there is still, in mid-1988, most room for criticism of details. One of the greatest anomalies was the treatment of banks by nationality. A British bank, for instance, would have needed to keep more capital against its exposure (over one year) to AAA-rated American than to B-rated British banks; an American bank would have had to keep the higher level against the AAA-rated British and lower against B-rated American banks. Fortunately, a late change treated all OECD banks alike, but still left a different treatment between OECD and non-OECD banks. Unless other anomalies are similarly ironed out by 1992, they will cause severe distortions in the market.)
(d) It makes a start towards establishing loan equivalents, under the name of risk equivalents.
(e) In the process of defining credit risk it in effect brings on balance sheet those items previously wrongly treated as off balance sheet.
(f) G10 itself nowhere mentions return on capital or risk; it should, however, make banks focus much more on the return they will need to service the appropriate levels of capital. This in turn should help to ensure that overall returns are sound, and that the returns on each product are sensible.

Overall therefore there can been little doubt that the ideas behind G10 are sound, and that at least the stronger banks will benefit from them.

There are three areas where they may be damaging to some or all banks. One is if the G10 have got certain aspects of the regulations wrong. This may apply to all G10 countries or may be the result of some central banks taking misguided advantage of the areas of flexibility. Either way, it is possible that the result may be a less than completely level playing-field. This may either be between banks, which is the most likely result of a single central bank getting it wrong; or between products if the regulations restrict some products more than others. The most obvious example here is the risk equivalents; if some products carry higher capital requirements than the risk justifies, this will distort the relative costs of competing products.

The second is that some banks are currently well below the levels of capital required. Although they have until 1992, reaching the full requirement will not be easy and this may force banks to lose business that they regard as desirable. Nevertheless, if the levels of capital required are generally about right, as the author of this book believes they are, this apparent sacrifice should be in the long-term interests of the banks concerned.

Finally there is a danger of excessive and expensive bureaucracy. To calculate the levels of capital needed and track them to ensure that a bank meets the requirements of its regulator will be time consuming, require large systems efforts, and a control system over actual exposure. Or at least it would need all that if a bank did not have something similar in place to manage its business already; it may need it anyway if the regulators insist on too rigid a format so that banks have to use special reporting systems for the regulators which do not help them manage their business. If that happens banks will need dual systems at great expense and probably some cost to the quality of management. If the regulators can avoid that trap, they will only be asking banks to do what they should do anyway to manage their business effectively.

In brief, if the regulators get any part of the approach wrong, then that could be a curse to all banks. It is important therefore that they listen to representations on points of detail now, and even more when the regulations have been in force for a while, generating experience of the way they work. With this proviso, however, the G10 rules seem likely to be much more of a blessing than a curse.

ONLY THEMSELVES TO BLAME

There will of course be some banks who suffer even if the regulations prove as near 100 per cent correct as can reasonably be expected.

These are the banks who have knowingly, or through ignorance or incompetence, operated on capital which was too small for the size and risks of their business; those which have been so obsessed with size or league tables that they have taken on business at silly returns or with little regard to risk, let alone risk/reward ratios; those who have allowed costs to get out of hand or mismanaged themselves in other ways. It almost goes without saying that these have only themselves to blame.

Then there are some banks which will claim that their capital is really sound but it is in a different form than G10 requires, or that it is in the form of hidden reserves. The Japanese, with their large unrealized profits on securities, are in the first category. They are allowed to count part of these gains, but less than they want. However, if they were to realize the gains, what was left after paying tax would count as capital. Of course if the Japanese banks all tried to realize at the same time the prices of the shares might fall, risking elimination of the unrealized gains. This is, after all, a major reason for not counting them as part of capital. Where the problem is hidden reserves, there is nothing to stop banks disclosing them. As far as the author is aware no country has any law forbidding the disclosure of hidden reserves. So in a slightly different sense these banks have only themselves to blame for the specific problems G10 may cause them.

Finally there is a risk that the view expressed above, that G10's proposals are broadly right, proves too optimistic. Even then, if the G10 regulators are quick to recognize this and correct the mistakes the impact may not be serious. But if G10 becomes rigid and unable to make adjustments to correct mistakes or meet changing conditions, all banks will have a major problem.

Even here, however, the banking system as a whole has only itself to blame. Government actions have caused or contributed to many of the mistakes banks have made. Some governments' efforts to dissociate themselves from the results of these mistakes can only be called unedifying. Nevertheless, whether it succeeds or not, G10 is clearly trying to push banks in the direction they ought to go and some have already gone. The fact that governments have to push, and that some banks find it hard to move along that path, is in the end the fault of bank managements rather than anybody else.

Index